Relational Discipleship

Relational Discipleship

Moving Back Home with God

BRIAN CRAIG DRUREY

WIPF & STOCK · Eugene, Oregon

RELATIONAL DISCIPLESHIP
Moving Back Home With God

Copyright © 2017 Brian Craig Drurey. All rights reserved. Except for brief quotations in critical publications or reviews, no part of this book may be reproduced in any manner without prior written permission from the publisher. Write: Permissions, Wipf and Stock Publishers, 199 W. 8th Ave., Suite 3, Eugene, OR 97401.

Wipf & Stock
An Imprint of Wipf and Stock Publishers
199 W. 8th Ave., Suite 3
Eugene, OR 97401

www.wipfandstock.com

PAPERBACK ISBN: 978-1-5326-1551-1
HARDCOVER ISBN: 978-1-5326-1553-5
EBOOK ISBN: 978-1-5326-1552-8

Manufactured in the U.S.A.   FEBRUARY 2, 2017

Scripture quotations marked (NIV) are taken from the Holy Bible, New International Version®, NIV®. Copyright © 1973, 1978, 1984, 2011 by Biblica, Inc.™ Used by permission of Zondervan. All rights reserved worldwide. www.zondervan.com The "NIV" and "New International Version" are trademarks registered in the United States Patent and Trademark Office by Biblica, Inc.™

Scripture quotations marked (ESV) are from The Holy Bible, English Standard Version® (ESV®), copyright © 2001 by Crossway, a publishing ministry of Good News Publishers. Used by permission. All rights reserved.

Scripture quotations noted (CEB) are taken from the Common English Bible, copyright © 2011. Used by permission. All rights reserved.

To my parents,
Don and Judy Drurey,
who taught me what
love looks like lived out
and where home could be found.

Contents

Acknowledgments | ix

Introduction | 1
1. God and Creation | 13
2. Grace—God's Love in Action | 28
3. Hospitality—Grace Expressed, Received, and Shared | 42
4. The Class Meeting—Help for the Journey Back Home | 66
5. One Step at a Time | 90
6. The Woods | 116
7. The Porch | 129
8. The Door | 140
9. The House | 150

Appendix A   The General Rules and Rules of the Band-Societies | 169
Appendix B   Rules of the Band-Societies | 172
Bibliography | 175

Acknowledgments

THIS BOOK HAS BEEN a lifetime in the making. In some ways, this book could be read as an autobiography. What I attempt to layout and describe in the following pages reflect much of my journey and the journey I am still on. Many people have been instrumental in both who I am today and in helping this book develop. First, I have to express my great appreciation for Dawn and Russell Morton, who tirelessly and diligently served as an editor and doctoral advisor respectively. Their wise input and words of encouragement are truly what made this endeavor even possible. I really don't think I would be typing these words right now had it not been for their help along the way.

Another person that made this project possible is Thomas Jay Oord. After some difficult years, I ended up in a theology class he was teaching at Northwest Nazarene University. It was during the pursuit of my Master of Divinity that my spiritual journey began to deepen and flourish like never before. Specifically, though, it was a theological paradigm shift in Oord's class that became the greatest catalyst. It was in this class that God became more personal and involved in my moment to moment living. Actually, it wasn't that God became more active, but my awareness of God's activity grew.

Since this class, Oord has become a good friend and a mentor. He has always made himself available to answer questions, offer advice, and provide challenging new ways to look at God, life, and theology. In fact, his most recent book, *The Uncontrolling Love of God: An Open and Relational Account of Providence*, has spurred even greater growth and movement toward God. Again, in many ways, this book is a reflection and a result of my journey intersecting with the teaching, writing, and friendship of Tom Oord.

I could not conclude my remarks without acknowledging another good friend and mentor, Raynard Martin. It was during this same time that I was taking Oord's class that Martin became both my pastor and mentor. If it had not been for Martin's encouragement and walking the journey with me during this theological paradigm shift, I may have never embraced these challenging ideas and made them my own. Martin listened well, spoke like a brother, and was faithfully present during this time. He truly has a pastor's heart and lives out his theology in a very practical way.

Since then, I have had the real pleasure and joy of serving in the church with him and putting this theology of God to work in real ways. He remains a good friend who is not afraid to listen to some of my crazy questions and ideas on theology. He remains a balance to my often extreme ways of thinking. Again, this book is in a large part a reflection of his friendship, example, and influence in my life.

Truly, the people I have mentioned above and many more that I cannot list in this short space, have contributed to who I am now and to the thoughts I have penned on the following pages. I am not over exaggerating when I say this book could never have been without them. As you continue your reading, keep in the back of your mind how this work is in some way a reflection of my journey and the contribution of these good people.

Introduction

A Longing for Home

I CAN REMEMBER GOING to visit my grandparents as a young child. My older brother and I would often go and spend several days with them. Occasionally grandma and grandpa would pick us up from our home, but most of the time mom and dad would take us to our grandparents. Mom and dad would stay and visit a short while and then the dreaded time for them to leave would come.

I loved my grandparents, and I did enjoy spending time with them. However, I would always miss mom and dad very much. The anticipation of the time when mom and dad would leave was always in the back of my mind. It would lay heavy on my heart, knowing that the moment would come when I would have to kiss mom and dad goodbye, and watch them pull out of the driveway. The moment I saw them pull out of the driveway, is the moment I felt all alone. I felt very far from home, and I longed to go back home. Paralyzed with heavy emotions, I would stand on the porch, crying because I missed mom and dad so much.

Fortunately, I eventually would get over the heavy feeling of missing home and would be able to enjoy staying with my grandparents. However, there was always a longing to go back home. As each day passed, the anticipation grew of seeing mom and dad again and being able to return home. It seemed as if there was an internal desire or compass built within me to return home.

A similar story occurred with my brother's family. My brother was raising three of his children when he remarried. Our family was raised and continues to live in Northeastern Ohio while my brother's new wife lived in New York. When my brother remarried, he decided to move himself and the children to New York with his new wife. It was a sad day when my brother and his three children moved away from their roots and home in Ohio.

Over the next couple of years, my brother and his family would come back to Ohio to visit. Everyone always looked forward to these visits as we watched the children getting bigger and older. Life was changing, but we always remembered what it is was like to have the family back together—to come back home. During this period, mom got sick and passed away. Mom's passing was very difficult for all of us and brought us even closer together as a family.

Shortly after mom's passing, my brother and his wife decided to follow his wife's parents, who had recently moved to Texas. If I were to guess, I would say that my brother's wife was experiencing the same longing we had—a longing for home. However, home was no longer in New York but home had moved to Texas where her parents had relocated. This move took my brother and his children even farther from Ohio.

We tried to stay in contact with my brother's family. We used social media, email, and phone. Regardless, they still seemed so far away. Unfortunately, my brother and his wife had a falling out, and they eventually divorced. What is remarkable is what occurred over the next several months after the divorce. First, my brother's oldest daughter moved back to Ohio. Then, his next oldest daughter moved back to Ohio. After some discussion, my brother and his son moved back to Ohio. There was a hunger, a desire, a compass pulling the children and my brother back to Ohio—back home.

I think most people can resonate with this inner longing for home. While I recognize that some home situations are not ideal and may have been abusive, people have a keen desire to belong somewhere they can call home. There is an innate homing beacon or compass that pulls and lures people to a place where they feel at home.

A Spiritual Home

Just as we long for a physical home, we have a spiritual homing beacon that is compelling us to find our spiritual home. Again, regardless of who we are and our past experiences, there is a compelling call in each of us to find our spiritual home. Each of us responds to this call differently: some by hiding, others by searching every nook and cranny, and yet others, by replacing

Introduction

home with other temporary housing which they erect to attempt to satisfy this desire for a spiritual home.

Jesus tasked the church with the purpose of teaching, enabling, and leading people back home to God. In Matthew 28:19, Jesus identified this process as making disciples. Over the history of the church, the body of Christ has experienced both success and failure in its ability to make disciples. The process of making disciples has looked different in each generation as modes, methods, and focus have changed over time.

Discipleship Today

I would like to take a snapshot of the state of discipleship in the church today. But before I continue, I would like to preface my remarks by clarifying that my evaluation is not meant to criticize the church but to think critically about how we are performing at our job of helping people come home to God. Additionally, I want to go on record by recognizing that discipleship and transformation do occur at some level today. However, in my evaluation, I am asking if we can improve our performance. Greg Boyd suggests, "If the church is to be the witness God calls us to be we must be ruthlessly honest with ourselves about the areas in which we are not where God wants us to be."[1] My intent is to look frankly at the current state of discipleship in the church today and ask if we may be able to find more faithful ways to disciple.

Dietrich Bonhoeffer has written that discipleship means following Christ in all ways.[2] Today, the term discipleship is used to describe an array of church functions and programs. American evangelicalism has reduced the implementing of this adherence to Christ to attending church, Sunday School, and other church programs, having private daily devotions, and receiving pastoral care from an ordained elder.[3] The church communicates that effective discipleship occurs while attending, sitting, and listening.[4] American discipleship has evolved into practices that do not demand

---

1. Boyd, *Repenting*, 45.

2. Hull, *Complete*, 15. Also, the primary reference remains an essential reference for discipleship with Bonhoeffer's distinction between "cheap grace" and costly grace. Bonhoeffer, *The Cost of Discipleship*, 45.

3. Hunter, *Radical*, 72.

4. Ibid., 72.

transformation but rather seeks personal and social fulfillment.[5] In reality, discipleship is often turned into a "personal choice or preference."[6]

Practical Atheism

There are two predominant paths of discipleship in today's American church.[7] The first pattern looks at discipleship as a matter of teaching biblical truths or propositions. While I approach this mode of discipleship frankly, I will not suggest that teaching biblical truth is unimportant. My concern is how this mode places a premium on knowledge and certainty of faith against experiential, transformational, and relational components.

This approach suggests that transformation will occur as people acquire knowledge of theological truths. This belief suggests that orthodoxy (right beliefs) precedes orthopraxy (right actions) and orthokardia (right desires).[8] This focus on teaching truths has resulted in the formation of means of grace that support this pattern. Most American churches rely heavily on preaching and teaching as ways to propagate discipleship.

This reliance on preaching and teaching has developed liturgies and programs focused on the execution of these two particular means of grace. In today's church, we often find preaching to be the central component of worship services. Many additional events place a premium on the event of preaching—i.e. revivals, camp meetings, seminars, and retreats. Most churches today view preaching and the response to preaching as a primary discipleship tool.

Over time, Sunday School became the discipleship arm of the church. In Sunday School, people gather around a predetermined curriculum where the goal is for people to answer the questions of the curriculum correctly.[9] Through the use of curriculum, little emphasis is placed on accountable, measurable transformation. In these groups, a good teacher or discipler is one who can disseminate the curriculum in a meaningful way.

Beyond preaching in the worship services and the Sunday School, the church often supplements the discipleship program of the church by adding other small group activities that center around Bible studies or other

---

5. Watson, *Foreclose*, 21.
6. Ibid., 22.
7. Donahue and Robinson, *Building*, 74.
8. Clapper, *Heart*, 19.
9. Donahue and Robinson, *Tightrope*, 25.

book studies. Again, immediate transformation may occur but there is no emphasis on continued long-term transformation resulting from the particular studies.[10] In recent trends in American discipleship, people, in a sincere desire for discipleship, think that the answer is to begin another Bible study.[11]

The assumption of this discipleship model as mentioned earlier is to provide right beliefs. The assumption generates a model that if we can teach people the right views, beliefs, and doctrines then it will trickle down into people's actions and desires. Inadvertently, this mode of discipleship typically falls way short of its desired outcome. The same disciples who are being taught right beliefs begin to get their life from these beliefs instead of the Christ toward whom these beliefs point.[12] These disciples become easily afflicted when other Christians espouse views that do not conform to the doctrines of these disciples. The test for orthodoxy has increasingly included more beliefs creating greater division in the larger body of Christ. Christians are disagreeing more and more on what the essential beliefs of Christianity should be. Churches are being found to be less of a place where grace can be experienced because people outside of the church assume that to partake in God's grace requires them to accept all the right beliefs that a particular tribe teaches before they can experience God's grace. This negative effect occurs when disciples derive their life from the beliefs they hold more than they do from Christ.

This discipleship model creates an urgency to attend classes and services. Meetings become the habit.[13] If there was a hunger for God in the beginning, the hunger is soon replaced with a hunger for knowledge, and/or guilt for not attending these meetings.[14] Again, I am not suggesting that meeting together is optional or that teaching and preaching are not helpful. However, I am suggesting that disciples in this mode are taught to exchange care for relationships with God and others for proper care of right beliefs. This lack of a proper level of right-relatedness results in "little intensity in confession, little delight in the gospel, little urgency in evangelism, little

---

10. Donahue and Robinson, *Tightrope*, 27.
11. Watson, *Class Meeting*, 78.
12. Boyd, *Benefit of the Doubt*, 66.
13. Carson, *Conversant*, 50.
14. Carson, *Conversant*, 50.

compassion for others, little humility in our evaluations, and little awareness of the authentic presence of God."[15]

This inadequate understanding of discipleship often stems from a congregation's misunderstanding about the nature of the atonement. Without getting into a lengthy theological discussion surrounding atonement theories, propositional based discipleship typically results from a view of salvation that is restricted by and large to the forgiveness of sins.[16] When atonement is seen as more of a legal arrangement providing for future eternal salvation, the urgency for real transformation in this life becomes less of a priority and potentially optional. This concept of salvation leads to failing to apply the Bible significantly and to live as citizens of the kingdom of God in this life.[17] As a result, a credibility gap ensues between how a disciple ought to live and how the disciple actually lives.[18]

John Wesley and other ministry practitioners have coined this credibility gap as practical atheism.[19] The practical atheist believes in the existence of God, but the belief results in little or no difference in the actions of the believer. I am not suggesting that right beliefs, Bible studies, preaching, and Sunday School are not important in the formation of disciples. I am suggesting that when the church disseminates right beliefs without any accountable discipleship, people will acquire head knowledge, but no significant transformation in desires and actions.

Fabs Harford shares that when we reduce discipleship to knowing things about God, we will find that we are producing disciples that look like demons.[20] They have perfect knowledge of God but lack relational knowledge of God. We read in the Bible, "You believe that there is one God. Good! Even the demons believe that—and shudder" (James 2:19 NIV). According to this scripture reference, demons are responding to their knowledge of God on a deeper level than some disciples who are focused on knowing right beliefs about God. The demons have enough respect for their knowledge of God to at least shudder!

---

15. Carson, *Conversant*, 50.
16. Carder and Warner, *Grace*, 56.
17. Donahue and Robinson, *Building*, 73.
18. Watson, *Blueprint*, 7. Also see N.T. Wright's *Paul and the Faithfulness of God* for a consideration of how justification and the atonement are not the same.
19. Carder and Warner, *Grace*, 19. Also see, J. Wesley, *The Works of John Wesley*, vol. 6, 28.
20. Harford, *Knowing God or Knowing about God*.

INTRODUCTION

Examples could be given how American Christians are acting no better than demons in the living out of their faith. Many of us have witnessed churches splitting over issues as simple as the style of worship and the color of the carpet. Another example is buying into extreme partisanship with the apparent need to choose one particular political party that is supposedly aligned with Christian views. Christians demonstrate "God's love" by their continual witch hunt for heretics and people who do not embrace a particular brand of Christianity. God's grace is dammed up when Christians choose to name one sin as being the deal breaker sin over the acceptable sins within a congregation. These examples and others demonstrate how truth based discipleship is only creating disciples that have knowledge of God without any meaningful transformation in living a life of love.

There is a significant credibility gap between what the Gospel proclaims and how many evangelical Americans live out their faith. This gap is tarnishing the witness of the church to a lost world. The world looks into the church and instead of seeing Jesus incarnate, sees Christians who espouse truth, acting in ways similar to how the world acts. Further, it is causing Christians who recognize this credibility gap in their lives either to participate marginally in the church, or worse, abandon their faith. Finally, children growing up under this kind of discipleship are abandoning the church.[21] This particular pattern of discipleship is at the root of what is hindering the church in its mission to the world.

Consumerism / Non-discipleship

The second pattern of discipleship is simply the option of non-discipleship.[22] In this option, people view discipleship as being reserved for the "super" Christian and only optional for most Christians.[23] Interestingly, a person's view of atonement significantly contributes to this particular approach to discipleship as well. Grace (I will argue an inadequate view of grace) and forgiveness become all that is necessary for Christians who are not of the super Christian variety.[24] This limited view of grace emphasizes that Christians are saved by grace, but this inadequate understanding of

---

21. Barna Group, "Six Reasons Young Christians Leave Church."
22. Boren, *Relational*, 230.
23. Hull, *Complete*, 16.
24. Ibid.

grace paralyzes further spiritual growth.[25] Participation in church ministries and programs become a matter of personal preference and taste. We can say that American consumerism takes precedence over serious spiritual formation.

When consumerism becomes the central emphasis in discipleship, the church, and any discipleship efforts become a "means to enhance private lives, self-esteem, and sense of purpose."[26] In this mode of discipleship, importance is not placed on relating rightly with God and others but instead priority is placed on personal enhancement and satisfaction. This selfish outlook demands that God, others, and the church meet and supply personal preferences and wants. Church and God become yet another service provider for the consumer's enjoyment. The Bible becomes only important in its ability to provide "quick answers" to immediate problems.[27] This pattern of discipleship results in "low commitment" from the participant and "non-invasive programming" from the church.[28]

Just as practical atheism resulting from knowledge-based discipleship has impacted the mission of the church, consumerism or non-discipleship also greatly impacts the witness and mission of the church in unique ways. Churches and Christians who submit to the pressure of consumerism produce and exhibit narcissistic traits in their followers.[29] Instead of disciples, these churches produce egotistic and self-absorbed followers. Egos and self-centeredness abound in these churches. People who do not get their way or who are not getting fed take the appropriate action of "listening to God's will" in finding a new flavor of church that will meet their needs.

Churches that are trying to demonstrate love and desire to meet the needs of the consumeristic disciple soon find their strength exhausted.[30] Resources and staff are poured into keeping the consumeristic disciple interested, fed, and engaged. Any slight yawn of this disciple, signifying a loss of interest in church programming, sends fear into the pastoral staff about how to satisfy and keep this disciple interested. Leaders of these churches chase the next big idea in church growth.

---

25. Hull, *Complete*, 16.
26. Boren, *Relational*, 94.
27. Ibid., 14.
28. Ibid.
29. Donahue and Robinson, *Tightrope*, 28.
30. Hull, *Complete*, 16.

Introduction

While consumeristic churches promote programs that appear relational, under the surface one finds that this paradigm is thoroughly "anti-relational."[31] This anti-relational core places the person at the center of importance.[32] Everyone and everything else become circles of influence around the person. The circles of influence are only acquaintances where people are not meaningfully related. People, in essence, are simply managing their "little kingdoms."[33] These little kingdoms only offer a sense of being relational because they are not emphasizing right-relatedness. Individuals experience what Scott Boren calls "crowded loneliness."[34] People feel like they have many friends because of the multiplicity of activities but in reality other people are just acquaintances.

Ultimately, with consumerism or non-discipleship everything is personal and all about the individual. The best one can hope for in this model is "private salvation, private discipleship, and private commitment."[35] There is no concern for loving God and others in biblical terms. The church and God can make no claim or call on the individual disciple because it boils down to a private or personal relationship.

Relational Discipleship

I have set out to describe the discipleship model I am advocating as "Relational Discipleship." In contrast to the two predominant patterns, I am proposing a more biblical, more satisfying model of discipleship. Some people may ask if the term relational discipleship is redundant. They ask, "How could discipleship be anything but relational?" I can understand their presumptions surrounding the combination of terms. While the components of relational discipleship are not new, it is not a predominant paradigm in the American church. Based on the two patterns of discipleship being predominantly practiced in American Christianity, I think we could conclude that authentic relational aspects are not always implied in today's discipling patterns.

Why do I choose to describe the focus of this resource as relational discipleship? Two central reasons come to mind. First, my particular lens

31. Boren, *Relational*, 73.
32. Ibid.
33. Ibid.
34. Ibid., 74.
35. Ibid., 75.

of theology can be described as relational. Relational theology can be summarized as an approach to theology that recognizes and emphasizes the relational qualities of God and creation. To consider relational theology from an introductory perspective, I recommend the book *Relational Theology: A Contemporary Introduction* edited by Brint Montgomery, Thomas Jay Oord, and Karen Winslow. So first, I recognize the influence of relational theology on the way I approach discipleship. Thus, relational discipleship derives its focus from relational theology.

My second reason for naming this model of discipleship relational is to emphasize the focus on doing discipleship as a community and a journey. As indicated in the current prevalent modes of discipleship, we can see that relational qualities have not been significantly important in mainstream evangelicalism. Adding to this is a second lens I approach theology with, my Wesleyan heritage. The theology and methodology of John Wesley are central to my understanding of ecclesiology and how we experience salvation today. As this resource unfolds, we will have an opportunity to see how John Wesley's model of discipleship places a premium on relational qualities.

As we begin to unpack relational discipleship, I will demonstrate how this pattern more closely resembles biblical and historical approaches to helping people find their way back to God and to move home with God. An example of this unfolds as we recollect the term "to know" in its Hebraic/biblical concepts. In Hebrew, we recognize that "to know" goes much further than our notions of "to know" today. As the first pattern of discipleship based on knowledge depicts, "to know" today refers to a cognitive level of knowledge. Thus, we see why that particular mode of discipleship focuses on cognitive knowledge of propositional truth and why disciples of this pattern are centrally interested in getting and espousing right doctrines. As I define relational discipleship, we will see that relational discipleship focuses on knowing, in "all ways that one knows and relates to another," both God and other people.[36]

As this resource on relational discipleship unfolds, we will see that relational discipleship is primarily concerned with experiencing what Greg Boyd calls "the unsurpassable worth God ascribes to us and in turn expressing that unsurpassable worth back to God, ourselves, and others."[37] In the Wesleyan tradition, we would call this perfect love. The goal of relational

---

36. Manskar, *Accountable*, 20.
37. Boyd, *Repenting*, 48.

Introduction

discipleship is this perfectly experienced and enacted love that can only begin with the love of God.[38]

This pattern of discipleship is relational in that it recognizes the presence of other unique individuals.[39] In knowledge-based discipleship, the premium is placed on truth. In consumeristic discipleship, the premium is placed on the individual. However, in relational discipleship significant value is placed on the other. God and other people become important and necessary relationships in this pattern of discipleship. Relational discipleship depends significantly on experiencing and relating to both God and others.[40]

These experiences of the other are dependent on the careful utilization of means of grace.[41] The means of grace (spiritual disciplines like prayer, Bible reading, worship, etc.) are opportunities to experience God or to remove barriers to experiencing God while at the same time interacting with other people. In other modes of discipleship, means of grace are enacted for personal benefit while, in relational discipleship, the means of grace are enacted to experience God and others in a meaningful way.

I believe both the church and the world today are hungry for a relational discipleship model. People are desiring for a connection between what they believe, why they believe, and how they behave in response to their beliefs. People are also hungry for connectedness. The days of private and individual experiences are gone. People want to belong. People want to be connected. They want their lives and actions to have meaning and purpose.

I have organized this resource on relational discipleship in a way that will build the relational discipleship house in a successive fashion. The first chapter will discuss God and creation. The purpose of this chapter is to lay a theological foundation for understanding why we need a relational discipleship focus. The second chapter proceeds to unravel the importance of a correct, optimistic understanding of God's grace. God's grace is the action that God takes that makes relational discipleship possible. In the following chapter, I will take grace and begin to describe grace as hospitality. As relational discipleship unfolds, we will see how viewing grace and

---

38. J. Wesley, "A Plain Account of Christian Pefection," *The Works of John Wesley*, vol. 11, 366. Also see "The Almost Christian," vol.5, 17 and "Christian Perfection," vol.6, 1.

39. Knight, *Presence*, 11.

40. Ibid.

41. Ibid., 13.

our response and cooperation with grace as hospitality to being essential in how we interact with God and others.

After I describe grace as hospitality, I will introduce the class meeting in the following chapter. In this chapter, I will provide some history of the Methodist class meeting and then proceed to describe how a re-traditioned class meeting for today becomes a way to help people experience and respond to God's hospitality. In the sixth chapter, I will introduce the concept of degrees of faith. This chapter will be important in helping the discipler see that while crisis experiences of God's grace are meaningful, there are also many smaller movements toward God in between the crisis experiences.

The final chapters take each segment of coming home to God and explores those areas in detail. The first movement is to become awakened in the woods or while living in the broken down shacks of life we have created. The next movement is defined as the porch of God. This porch is where people preveniently learn about God and are convinced of their need for God. The next chapter will discuss the door of God's house which can be described as justifying grace provided by the work of Jesus Christ. Finally, to move home and to live with God will be discussed as sanctifying grace.

I have always respected John Wesley for his approach to theology. He desired to communicate theology in ways that were helpful to ordinary people. He was known as a practical theologian in that his theology was all about being practiced and lived out.[42] As I attempt to unravel what I propose surrounding relational discipleship, I will inadvertently have to lay out some theological foundations. I hope to describe these theological concepts in accessible and practical ways. In fact, I will utilize story telling throughout the work to give one more tool to connect the theology and practical implications. The stories throughout the chapters build on one another and hopefully you can hear the connection between them.

I have already confessed upfront my Wesleyan and Relational lens. Wrestle with the theology as you may. Engage it, research it, and even pray about it. In the end, what matters is what you will do with Christ's challenge to you and the church to go and make disciples. Are you willing to examine relational discipleship as a potential resource to help you become a more effective discipler? Can you become more effective at helping people find their way home to God?

---

42. J. Wesley, "Preface," *The Works of John Wesley*, vol. 5, 2.

1

God and Creation

A Story to Set the Stage—God's Gracious Call to Home

I would like for us to begin by considering a story. At the start of this story, we find a mom and dad and their two youngest children, a teenage son and a teenage daughter. The dad is a very successful architect. People from all around want him to design their next building or house. His designs are beautiful, yet simple; practical, but elegant. In fact, the home that he and his family now live in was just recently designed by him and built with his family in mind.

Trevor, his son, is creative. He likes to take gadgets apart and redesign and repurpose them into something new. His dad knew how much Trevor loved to create and to work to come up with new ideas. When his dad designed this house, he even included a special work area for his son. He wanted his son to enjoy the home.

Sammy was the younger daughter. She also had her own interests. She always seemed to find hurting and abandoned animals: the stray cat; the baby bird that fell out of the nest; the dog that was hit by a car and left hurting along the road. Out of her love for animals, Sammy began volunteering at a veterinarian clinic. The vet saw how she liked to nurse animals back to health and recognized that space was limited at his clinic. Her father also became aware of this fact. As a result, he designed a little clinic on the back of the property for Sammy. It was convenient for the vet to make house calls and to give advice and check up on Sammy's work. Sammy was in heaven when she was helping these animals.

The whole family enjoyed the family room that dad designed for them. This room was a place where they enjoyed being together as a family. Dad's desire was to enjoy his family's presence. He knew this building was only a house, but he wanted to make this house feel like home so that Sammy and Trevor knew they belonged and were loved. Dad cherished the time he talked, read, and lived with Sammy and Trevor.

One weekend, mom and dad decided they would go on a trip. They knew that Sammy and Trevor were getting older and more responsible. They decided it would be safe to leave Sammy and Trevor by themselves. As they prepared for the trip, the parents made sure there were plenty of groceries and household items. When it was time to leave, mom and dad reiterated the house rules and house chores. They embraced their children and told them how much they loved Sammy and Trevor. The children then waved bye as they watched their parents drive off that Friday afternoon.

We are not sure whose idea it was first. All we know is that just hours after mom and dad left, a party had been planned. No parties were one of the house rules. They could each invite a friend over, but no party was permitted.

At ten that night, we find the party in full swing. Sammy and Trevor had no idea what they had gotten themselves into. Their sacred family area—where they enjoyed the family getting together was being torn apart- beverages spilled, trash all over, furniture knocked over, and things broke. How could Sammy and Trevor ever spend time with dad again in this room, seeing how they let it be destroyed? Their dad would be so disappointed if he were here. What will dad say when he gets back?

More tragedy took place during the party. Sammy decided to show a few of her friends her little clinic. What she did not know was that a bunch of people followed her. She couldn't control them: they opened cages, poked fingers, made faces, and loud noises. These helpless, hurt animals were being frightened. And as the cages were opened, the animals went running. What Sammy enjoyed doing was being distorted and ruined because of her and Trevor's decision to misuse and disobey dad's house rules.

The same happened to Trevor's special work area. A few friends ended up being a mob of people. They were picking up, handling, and dropping everything Trevor was working on—gadgets were broken, and things were missing and out of place. His work that he enjoyed became distorted and ruined.

The party ended early Saturday morning. Sammy and Trevor couldn't sleep. All they could do is look at the mess they had created by not following the house rules. They had no idea how they could get the house back in order before mom and dad came back home Sunday evening. They spent most of Saturday fighting back and forth about what to do and whose fault it was. As they looked around that evening, they recognized that little was accomplished. Being both exhausted from the sleepless night before and the fighting back and forth during the day, they finally collapsed in despair.

Sunday morning came quickly. Sammy and Trevor were awakened by the sound of the doorbell and ran down to see who it was. When they opened the door, they were surprised to see their older brother Jesse, who had been away at college, standing there. They embraced him like never before. Even though they knew the house was a mess, they were happy to see their older brother. Jesse could help out. Jesse could give them advice. Jesse could be a shoulder to cry on and confess to.

As they brought Jesse in, Jesse quickly saw what kind of mess the two had made of the home dad had created for them. Jesse decided to roll his sleeves up and work alongside Sammy and Trevor as they worked to put the house back in order. They worked and worked. It looked a whole lot better than when Jesse first got there. However, it still did not look like dad had originally intended it to be. It still did not feel like home. About this time, Jesse told Sammy and Trevor that he had to get going.

What they did not realize was that dad had sent Jesse from the very beginning to help Sammy and Trevor. Dad had received a phone call from one of the neighbors Friday night about the wreck the children were making out of the house. In his concern and love for his kids, he thought it would be best to send his older son—big brother to help out. He knew it would ease the pain and begin the reconciliation before he would return home.

They also did not know that Jesse was going back to dad. Jesse was going to share with dad the confession Sammy and Trevor shared and their desire to set things right. Dad knew what exactly was going on over the weekend. Dad's heart was broken, but dad knew Jesse could be counted on to help the younger siblings. Dad also knew that once he came back everything would be set right again.

Mom and dad did return home. They saw the remorse from Sammy and Trevor and how Sammy and Trevor tried to set things right. There was still brokenness. Animals were still missing and gadgets broken. Things just were not as they were intended. When dad walked up to Sammy and Trevor, he wiped the tears from their eyes and said dad is going to make everything new. We are going to get rid of the trash and restore all things back to how they were intended to be. Dad is home.

As we read this story, one can see similar attributes of a loving Heavenly Father. From Genesis 1 to Revelation 22, we see God acting in a similar way—from the perfect home God created for us in Genesis 1 and 2, to how we, the children, have destroyed the home God created. God created a good, beautiful home. A home that matched the image of God created in humans. We in turn messed up God's house and the original design and intent God created. We then see how the Father sent his Son, our older brother, Jesus to help us see what the original home looked like. Then, to the Son going back to the Father. And finally, God coming back home and living with the children, restoring all things back to their original beauty, order, and intent. Dad is home in Revelation 21 and 22.

We often think about going to heaven. There is a significant amount of discussion in Christian circles about what happens when we die. Some Christians believe we fall asleep till the Second Coming. Others say we go to heaven. Others say we go to something like heaven, but it is a waiting area until Christ returns.[1] My intent is not to solve this debate in this work. I do believe that there is somewhere in God's presence we go if we have accepted the salvation God has provided. Call it heaven . . . or paradise, whatever you may like. We do know that Paul said that to die is to be with God (2 Corinthians 5:8). For simplicity sake, let us just call it heaven. For our consideration, we are not talking about what happens when we die.

We are talking about the culmination of time, what many people refer to as Jesus coming again. What will that look like? Again, there are many opinions and debates about how and what that will look like. Instead, we will consider Revelation 21. If we are to read this passage faithfully, it does not sound like that at the end we are going to heaven. But in the end, it sounds like heaven is coming to earth. Let us consider this passage:

Revelation 21 Common English Bible (CEB)

> 21 Then I saw a new heaven and a new earth, for the former heaven and the former earth had passed away, and the sea was no more.
> 2 I saw the holy city, New Jerusalem, coming down out of heaven

---

1. Howard Snyder considers the notion of falling asleep in his blogpost. Howard Snyder, "Do Christians Fall Asleep?" For further treatment, consider this blog entry: Warren Prestidge, "Asleep in Christ: The Death State."

from God, made ready as a bride beautifully dressed for her husband. 3 I heard a loud voice from the throne say, "Look! God's dwelling is here with humankind. He will dwell with them, and they will be his peoples. God himself will be with them as their God. 4 He will wipe away every tear from their eyes. Death will be no more. There will be no mourning, crying, or pain anymore, for the former things have passed away." 5 Then the one seated on the throne said, "Look! I'm making all things new." He also said, "Write this down, for these words are trustworthy and true." 6 Then he said to me, "All is done. I am the Alpha and the Omega, the beginning and the end. To the thirsty I will freely give water from the life-giving spring.

God has always desired to live with God's people. God finally gets what God wants—to live in God's unrestricted presence with God's people. It also sounds like all of God's creation is important to God. Allow me to share some other scripture references:

Matthew 19:28 New International Version (NIV):"28 Jesus said to them, 'Truly I tell you, at *the renewal of all things*, when the Son of Man sits on his glorious throne, you who have followed me will also sit on twelve thrones, judging the twelve tribes of Israel.'"

Acts 3:21 Common English Bible (CEB): "21 Jesus must remain in heaven until *the restoration of all things*, about which God spoke long ago through his holy prophets."

Colossians 1:20 Common English Bible (CEB):

20 and he *reconciled all things* to himself through him—
whether things on earth or in the heavens.
He brought peace through the blood of his cross.

Romans 8:18-25 Common English Bible (CEB):

18 I believe that the present suffering is nothing compared to the coming glory that is going to be revealed to us. 19 *The whole creation* waits breathless with anticipation for the revelation of God's sons and daughters. 20 Creation was subjected to frustration, not by its own choice—it was the choice of the one who subjected

> it—but in the hope 21 that the creation itself will be set free from slavery to decay and brought into the glorious freedom of God's children. 22 We know that *the whole creation* is groaning together and suffering labor pains up until now. 23 And it's not only the creation. We ourselves who have the Spirit as the first crop of the harvest also groan inside as we wait to be adopted and for our bodies to be set free. 24 We were saved in hope. If we see what we hope for, that isn't hope. Who hopes for what they already see? 25 But if we hope for what we don't see, we wait for it with patience.

Do you know what the Greek word is for all things? Are you ready? It is *all things!* Do you hear these words? Jesus said the renewal of all things ... Acts talks about the restoration of all things ... Colossians discusses the reconciling of all things ... and finally Paul talks about how all of creation is groaning and awaiting the time of being set free from the slavery of decay that humanity has brought on to creation.

From these verses and Revelation 21, we hear a God that is not abandoning God's creation, but a God, who comes from heaven to earth, to live in God's unrestricted presence. By this very unrestricted presence, God makes all things new. God's kingdom finally comes without the old ways impeding the kingdom. God takes the trashy old things out and makes everything new. For God, salvation is not about personal fire insurance for an individual but salvation for God is about redeeming, reconciling, and making all things new. God's desire is to set home up right like God originally intended it to be. None of us can be certain what this potential end time will look like or how it will come. However, it does sound like God is interested and at work to redeem, reconcile, renew, and restore.

Scripture is God's story. The story of God creating home in the very beginning. It was a good home; God said so. God created what humanity needed to be satisfied and to live with God. Humanity decided to rebel and throw a party. Humanity made a wreck of the home God created. Scripture is God's story of God trying to reach humanity and set home back right. Scripture tells us that God the Father sent his Son—our older brother to demonstrate what living in the Father's home looks like. Our older brother even died to help the other children see the Father's love for them. And, scripture describes that somehow and sometime, Dad will come home and set everything right, make everything new. But in the meantime, our older Brother taught us this:

(Matthew 6:9–13).

Our Father, which art in heaven,
Hallowed be thy Name.
Thy Kingdom come.
Thy will be done in earth,
as it is in heaven.
Give us this day our daily bread.
And forgive us our trespasses,
As we forgive those that trespass against us.
And lead us not into temptation,
but deliver us from evil.
For thine is the kingdom, the power, and the glory,
Forever and ever. Amen.

We pray for the kingdom of God to come. We pray that God's will be done here on earth as it is in heaven. While we wait for the return of Jesus Christ, while we wait for Dad to come and live among us in God's unrestricted presence, while we wait for the full coming of the kingdom of God, it is our responsibility to pray, to live, and to bring the kingdom of God as much as we are humanly possible. John the Baptist and Jesus both proclaimed that the kingdom of God is here. While it is not fully intact, while their seems to be a spirit of anti-Christ influencing governments, institutions, ways of thinking, ways of living, ways of being—we the Body of Christ are to live in the kingdom of God—to be counter-cultural to unloving ways of being.

The only way we can live as the kingdom of God in this world is to live in an awareness of God's presence now. Let us live in God's presence at this moment—to remain in God's presence or to dwell in God's presence. God's presence is what changes, transforms, and makes everything new.

Theological Implications

As I indicated in the Introduction, I admitted that I would have to discuss some theological foundations in order to understand the relational framework that I would construct. Again, I am not trying to convey deep theological understandings but provide the necessary foundation for the practical implications. My aim is to reveal the theological lens from which I operate so that it may provide a clearer, practical outcome for those disciplers that find relational discipleship to be a compelling pattern.

I often cringe when I hear someone remark, "The Bible clearly says" or "Just follow scripture." On many instances, what people are really saying is "My interpretation is the correct interpretation of the Bible." As I approach these theological underpinnings, I clearly confess my lens. My hope is that the preliminary story and scriptures I have shared at the beginning of this chapter will set the tone and provide illumination as I attempt to consider what is assumed theologically in order to progress in a relational discipleship model. I do not claim my particular views to be the only way to view scripture and theology. I do believe that my Relational and Wesleyan lenses are faithful to an orthodox Christian view and within a faithful understanding of a Protestant and especially a Wesleyan approach to scripture and theology.

The Trinity

It would not be theology (the study of God) unless we started with a consideration of God and especially a Trinitarian view of God. One way of describing the Trinity from an orthodox perspective suggests the Trinity consists of the Father, the Son, and the Holy Spirit interacting within community. The Trinity has been an eternally existent "small group."[2] This Trinity has been eternally exhibiting love and creating community among the three persons. The whole concept of God being a community of three distinct divine persons yet one God is crucially important to the whole relational discipleship model. When we say that God created people in God's image, we are saying "at least in one way the image is exhibited in us is in the gathering and the mutual benefit of a small group."[3] We cannot understand and define an orthodox view of God apart from community.[4] We understand God as a relational small group.

This Trinitarian small group could not exist if God was not love. For God to be in perfect relational interaction within the Trinity, love must be at the heart and essence of who God is.[5] The Trinity perfectly displays a self-emptying love between the persons of the Trinity and creation.[6]

---

2. Donahue and Robinson, *Building*, 22.
3. Ibid.
4. Ibid.
5. Boyd and Eddy, *Across*, 82.
6. Lodahl, *Nature*, 97. Also see, Thomas Jay Oord, *The Uncontrolling Love of God*, 159. Oord argues that a more helpful way of defining *kenōsis* is self-giving love.

While we can say God is omnipotent, God has demonstrated that God does not "hoard power."[7] For any member of the Trinity, the use of coercive power over another member would be opposite of who God is. God has demonstrated that the way God influences and interacts within the Trinity and with creation is through self-emptying love. John Wesley indicated that God's sovereignty should never be spoken of apart from God's reigning attribute of love.[8] We can say that God never does anything because God is sovereign but always from God's love.[9] We could clarify it this way, "God rules in love but does not love to rule."[10]

This self-emptying love that God is and exhibits takes us toward an understanding of God as a relational community who desire to enter and create a relational creation. We describe God's self-emptying love in interaction with creation as grace. Anything that God does to interact and influence God's creation can be categorized as grace. As opposed to a Calvinistic understanding of grace, a Wesleyan lens understands that grace is *not* irresistible. Grace can be rejected or accepted. Because of God's desire to be relationally interacting with creation, "relational vulnerability exists."[11] The risk God takes to love opens God up to rejection and suffering.[12]

This self-emptying love defines another attribute of God. We understand God to be omnipresent. We often think God is somewhere else, but in reality God is "closer to you and I than we can realize."[13] Acts 17:28 reminds us that we live, move, and have our being in God. God is radically with us and being a "present influence" on us in each moment.[14] In this always present condition, "our decisions and actions impact God and genuinely make a difference in God's response to us."[15] In each moment, God is always present, acting first in grace or self-emptying love toward us.[16]

---

7. Lodahl, *Nature*, 97.

8. Clark H. Pinnock, *Grace Unlimited*, (Eugene, OR: Wipf and Stock Publishers, 1998), 212.

9. Ibid., 75. We also hear the same importance on the centrality of God's love in Mildred Bangs Wynkoop's writing. Mildred Bangs Wynkoop, *A Theology of Love*, 14.

10. Ibid., 75.

11. Pinnock, *Grace*, 92.

12. Ibid.

13. Lodahl, *Nature*, 113.

14. Stone and Oord, *Name*, 73.

15. Stone and Oord, *Name*, 73.

16. Ibid., 99.

Always Creating Home

We can take this always present, self-emptying love called grace a step further and suggest that God has always been about creating home.[17] Genesis 1 and 2 faithfully depict God's original intent for the creation God created. The creation account describes God's desire to create a "good" home for all of creation. God's original design for home was for all created life to relate well with each other and their Creator. In God's relationship to creation, God has always had steadfast love when relating to creation.[18] We can place our confidence in this unchanging aspect of God. God's character will always be that of love toward God's creation and therefore always creating and calling creation home.

As we progress throughout scripture, we find that every divine activity proceeds from God's self-emptying love and works toward making home.[19] We can see that the Bible contains "household language" as it attempts to describe how God and people relate.[20] For instance, God's original design for creation was a "well-designed living space."[21] We read how God first set up this well-designed living space in the creation account of Genesis.[22] God acts in ways that display God's self-emptying love as God creates, provides, and calls creation home.

In God creating home to be relational, where creation could lovingly interact with God and others, God's nature called for freedom to either cooperate with God's grace or to reject God's grace. We call this ability to relate—free will. For home to be a place where love is mutually experienced, God took a risk. Anytime a relationship is entered; risk is involved. The love that God is—commits to creation knowing the potential cost and the suffering that could occur.[23] In this posture, God's love cannot be controlling or manipulative. God in love, gives us the opportunity to decide how to respond to God's love.[24] The degree with which God loves, God cannot love creation any more than God already does. God's great love opened God

---

17. Oord, *Love*, 138. Here Oord argues that "God everlastingly creates."
18. Blevins and Maddix, *Discovering*, 57.
19. O'Connell, *Compassion*, 65.
20. Manskar, *Accountable*, 32.
21. Boyd, *Repenting*, 69.
22. Boyd, *Repenting*, 69.
23. Boren, *Relational*, 32.
24. Ibid.

up to a great level of suffering. This love of God is what compels God to be always creating home for God's creation.

The Children Mess Home Up

God created home knowing full well the risk God was taking. Genesis 3 describes what happens when humanity chooses not to cooperate lovingly with God's grace. The story in Genesis 3 depicts, through Adam and Eve, how when we live in isolation from God and others we cease to be "fully human."[25] When we live in this perceived isolation, we begin to act in ways that reject the distinctive other. Our lives become imbalanced in that we place the source of our life on other things than God.[26] Either things or ourselves become the center of our lives. In this imbalanced living—sin, death, chaos, destruction, and disorder result in the home God creates.

The knowledge of good and evil that is alluded to in the Genesis 3 account of the children messing the house up refers to our desire to judge good and bad, right and wrong, in others and the perceived feeling of being judged by others.[27] In this place of judging, shame and hiding result as people live outside the house or presence of God.[28] The story of Adam and Eve reveals what happened when people began living in this isolation; they hid from God for fear of God's judgment. They also clothed themselves, effectively hiding themselves from each other's judgmental attitude. With this inclination toward judgment, or as we call it—original sin, people are alienated from God's presence and from living well with others and God's creation.[29]

This inclination to judge others results in us fearing judgment from God and others. This fear propagates the disconnection from God and from whom we are meant to be.[30] We can see how fear precedes hate. Our alienation has created fear within us and causes us to act in non-loving ways to both God and others. As we live out of this fear, we make decisions that result in not relating well with God and others. This fear causes us to place our interests and concerns before God and others. Instead of reflect-

25. Boyd and Eddy, *Across*, 82.
26. Boyd, *Repenting,* 69.
27. Boyd, *Repenting,* 160.
28. Ibid., 159.
29. Ibid., 17.
30. Wolsey, "A Progressive Christian View of Sin and Sinners."

ing the self-emptying love that the Triune God displays, we live out of a selfish, self-centered love. All of this self-centered love makes a mess out of God's original home.

Our Older Brother

As God would do, God acts in the most loving ways possible to interact and invite creation to come back home to God and to live again in ways that enable each other to flourish. In Jesus, the Son of the Trinity, coming to live among people, to die, and to be resurrected back to life, there is nothing more God could have done than God did in this act to express God's love for creation.[31] God went to the furthest extremes to span the alienation we created when we began to choose not to cooperate with God's grace. The Son, Jesus, through self-emptying love, spanned the perceived alienation we created through our judgment and fear of judgment. In Jesus' innocence, we judged Jesus and put to death the only one not deserving to be judged. Jesus accepted our judgment and all the violence, blame, and sin we could throw at Jesus. He went to this great length to demonstrate the extent of God's love for creation. Jesus had to go to this extreme to prove that our judgment about God had been wrong all along. The alienation we had been experiencing was not caused by God distancing God from us, but us hiding in fear from God.

We see in Jesus' living among us, a desire for God to be known in the deeper Hebraic sense I referred to in the Introduction. God has never wanted people to know just propositional truths about God. Steven Manskar says it well, "God desires to know and to be known in all the ways that one knows and relates to each other."[32] Jesus says in John 14:9 that when we see Jesus, we have seen the Father. How Jesus lived, loved, interacted, died, and was raised to life reflects who the Father is. From the birth of Jesus to the ascension of Jesus, we can "get to know" God more intimately.

In the teachings and life of Jesus, our older Brother has come to the house the Father created, and that the children have made a mess of. In our older Brother coming to the house, our older Brother has begun the work of setting the house back in order—to its original design and intent. We often refer to this beginning of setting things back in order as the coming of the kingdom of God. Restoration and reconciliation for all of creation are

31. Boyd, *Repenting*, 27.
32. Manskar, *Accountable*, 20.

the purpose of our older Brother's first advent to the house. Jesus came to begin the work of cleaning up the mess humanity has made of God's house. Jesus lovingly invites us to cooperate in this setting this house right—the coming of the kingdom of God.

God's Desire to Restore the Image

God understands that for people to be able to cooperate in helping to set the house back in order, our deformed image of God in us needs to be healed. The Wesleyan way of salvation has a helpful way of perceiving how God initiates and enables this healing to take place in those people's lives who choose once again to cooperate with God's grace.

John Wesley understood God's grace to be only one grace.[33] However, to help people understand the transformation of our broken images back into reflecting God's image of perfect love, Wesley broke grace down into measurable experiences and responses to God's grace.[34] First, Wesley understood all grace to be prevenient in that *all* grace *always* precedes *any* action on our part.[35] So, every step toward God is first enabled by God's gracious move.

Because our perceived alienation from God and others is so great, God must always take the first action or step toward us to overcome this alienation. Wesley considered this first movement of grace as prevenient grace as well.[36] This prevenient grace is what enables a person to become aware or awakened to God and the things of God. This first movement of grace also helps one become aware of one's alienation—sin (state of being) and one's awareness of relating to others and God poorly—sins (actions). In this state of prevenient grace, one learns there is hope for healing of both the sin and sins in one's life.

As God continues to act in grace, God will eventually invite one through the door of justifying grace. This justifying grace is the work of atonement that Christ completed entirely in his life, death, and resurrection

---

33. Harper, *The Way to Heaven*, 34. Also see J. Wesley, "On Working out Our Own Salvation," *The Works of John Wesley*, vol. 6, 508. Also see, Lodahl, *Nature*, 140.

34. J. Wesley, "A Plain Account of Christian Perfection," *The Works of John Wesley*, vol. 11, 383.

35. Wesley used the term "preventing grace." J. Wesley, "The Scripture Way of Salvation," *The Works of John Wesley*, vol. 6, 44.

36. J. Wesley, "The Scripture Way of Salvation," *The Works of John Wesley*, vol. 6, 44.

for all of creation. When one enters this door of justifying grace, one becomes aware of her status as being a child of God all along. The perceived alienation is confronted with the truth of the work of Christ. As the person becomes aware of her place as a child of God, gratitude swells up for God. In later chapters, we will develop how gratitude is always the proper response to grace and how a cycle of grace fuels discipleship.[37]

God's grace does not stop there. God desires for all the effects of the alienation to be healed and overcome. This alienation is healed as one begins to live continually in the house of God—or to live in the presence of God moment by moment. 1 John 4:18 explains that perfect love casts out fear. As we experience the perfect love of God as we live moment by moment in God, the fear that was created by our perceived alienation is cast out. We then begin loving in this similar way that we have experienced from God and others. Wesley called this grace sanctifying grace. This living in God's presence is what heals and transforms the image of God that has been deformed by the alienation.

This process of healing the deformed image of God in our lives so that we can help bring the kingdom of God, or help clean the house up, is called discipleship. This task is what God has instructed the church to carry on. Discipleship is not about making sure we have fire insurance for eternity. Discipleship is not about teaching truths so we can hold the right doctrine and answer questions correctly. Discipleship is teaching people how to recognize and respond to God's grace in each moment so that the image of God's perfect love can be restored in us so that we may be able to begin the process of cleaning the Father's house up here and now. It is when we can truly experience the love God has for us that we can begin to love God and others in the way God intends for us.

God Finally Gets What God Wants

Revelation 21 and 22 depicts the end of the story for God's desire to always create home. Full salvation will culminate when God brings heaven to earth (restores the Kingdom of God as it was intended to be).[38] In these last two chapters of Revelation, it appears that the kingdom of God finally fully comes to earth. Creation is healed, restored, made new, and reconciled. Salvation comes to all of creation. God restores home where no one is

37. Pohl, *Living*, 24.
38. Watson, *Foreclose*, 19.

excluded by the alienation and judgment of others who are not qualified to judge.[39] God provides abundant life to all of creation. The house is set back to its original design, purpose, and beauty. In this restored home, perfect love is mutually shared between the Triune God and creation. This home is the goal of salvation and discipleship is the process in this life toward that goal.

As we have seen in this chapter, God has always been creating and calling creation to home. God's reigning attribute of love desires to interact relationally with God's creation. In this desire to interact relationally, people were given free will that ultimately led people to choose ways that were not loving toward God and others. These choices have impacted the good creation God created. In God's love, Jesus came to begin the restoration of the home God created and that the children messed up. Additionally, God desires to help re-create God's likeness in us through discipleship. Finally, we see that God's salvation comes to all of creation when God's kingdom is fully set in place.

---

39. Meeks, *Economist*, 40.

2

Grace—God's Love in Action

God's Economy

IN THIS CHAPTER, I want to dig further into how we view grace. How we view grace determines how we perceive God, God's interaction with the world, and how we evangelize and disciple others. Grace is what makes discipleship and especially relational discipleship possible. As we begin to unpack the concept of grace, it will be important to keep the notion that God has always been about creating home central to our discussion. If we accept this notion, then we must wrestle with all the implications of creating and sustaining a household. An important place to begin with the sustaining of a home is the idea of economy. To understand God's grace, we first must take a look at God's economy. God's economy depicts the length at which God is involved in God's creation and ultimately God's interaction with human beings.

The Greek word from which we derive our word economy is *oikonomia*. This word is a compound of *oikos* meaning household and *nomos* meaning law or management.[1] From biblical times, we could infer that economy at its very roots dealt with the managing or taking care of the home.[2] Running the household would include "the production, distribution, and consumption of the necessities of life."[3] If we take seriously the notion that God has always been about creating home, then we must understand that there is an economy from which God operates or manages

---

1. "Greek Lexicon: G3622 (KJV)." Blue Letter Bible.
2. Meeks, *Economist*, 3.
3. Ibid.

the home. God is concerned with the home flourishing—not with only providing life but also quality of life.

Without going into political and economic discussions surrounding our day, I am confident that regardless of what side we come down on these beliefs, we all can recognize the shortcomings of secular governments and economies at providing and ensuring all people can flourish and have abundance of life. Our economies are focused on perceived and created notions of scarcity. Scarcity increases the economic value of those things that are perceived to be scarce, whether that be resources, labor, or whatever contribution is being considered. If a particular commodity has a great demand, without the output to provide an abundance of that demand, then that commodity increases in value and ultimately translates to a higher price for that commodity. People who have little means have limited ability to select and choose commodities for their home. Thus, scarcity impacts people and the ability of their homes to flourish.

Again, I am not asking anyone to adopt a particular political or economic view. However, I would like to compare and contrast typical world economic views with the economy of God and the Gospel. As mentioned, our economies are centered on the idea of scarcity. Scarcity is what causes people to hoard, to save more than they need, and to create judgments about other people. Within our economic structures, we often judge whether other people are deserving of the right to flourish. We make those judgments based on what we perceive of other people's behaviors like laziness, addictions, or greed. These judgments often incline us to withhold our resources.

On the other hand, the Gospel presumes abundance.[4] Jesus says in John 10:10 that he has come to give abundant life. In God's economy, there is abundance. One of the first concepts we must conclude about God's grace is that there is an abundance of grace. There is no reason to fear scarcity with God's grace. As this resource unfolds, I will suggest that at times the church blocks and dams up God's grace based on a worldly view of economy and scarcity.

We can further generalize world economic models by saying they focus on "the exchange of power and wealth, commodities, and self-identified needs."[5] Conversely, God's economy measures worth based on "relationship

---

4. Carder and Warner, *Grace*, 58.
5. Meeks, *Economist*, 7. Also see, Carder and Warner, *Grace*, 58.

to God and others and the intrinsic value of the other."[6] God's economy further values creating and gift giving over ownership and the consumption of commodities.[7] While world economies are concerned with equitable exchange, God's economy emphasizes "mutuality and shared gifts."[8] Finally, in God's economy, the focus is not on self-identified needs but rather on the "participation in God's mission emphasizing a self-emptying quality."[9]

All of these principles within God's economy are enabled by the notion of abundance. When there is abundance, there is no need for competition, judgment, and hoarding of resources, that stems from a false sense of scarcity. When people doubt either the abundance or the ability of grace, people naturally withhold sharing grace with people deemed too different, strange, or encumbering. If there is an abundance, then there is no need to withhold resources from those people deemed less valuable or less worthy. There is no fear because there is plenty of grace to go around. Only when we grasp the optimism of the vast abundance of God's grace will we be able to share this grace without fear or judgment of the people needing this grace.

In God's house, there is no scarcity.[10] When God is present, then there will always be plenty of grace to go around.[11] We can turn to scriptural accounts of God's presence for evidence of God's abundance and care for creation. Just to name a few examples, we find God supplying manna and water to the Israelites on their exodus from Egypt (Exodus 16). In this account, we find God present in the midst of Israel's struggle to be faithful to God. We also note the accounts of Jesus feeding the multitudes in the New Testament (Matthew 14:13–21). In this presence of God, we find once again abundance. We can also look to the feasts and celebrations that were instituted to celebrate God's goodness. Finally, an important act of abundance of God's grace can be found in our practice of the Eucharist. Jesus instituted this celebration as a time to both remember and to partake in God's good grace (Luke 22:7–23).

Interestingly, Jesus did not judge and withhold grace from the very people that would betray, deny, and run away from him that night. Jesus' grace was so abundant that he even willingly washed the feet of those very

---

6. Meeks, *Economist*, 11. Also see, Carder and Warner, *Grace*, 58.
7. Ibid., 119. Also see, Carder and Warner, *Grace*, 58.
8. Ibid., 34. Also see, Carder and Warner, *Grace*, 58.
9. Carder and Warner, *Grace*, 58.
10. Meeks, *Economist*, 12.
11. Ibid.

same people (John 13:1–17). Just as Jesus did, when God is present, we do not have to fear that our holiness is too fragile, or fear scarcity, to endure the challenge by sins we think are too great. We will find that this abundance in God's house is a key to what I will develop in the next chapter regarding hospitality.

As the example of abundance in God's house develops our understanding of hospitality, we will see, that in both the example of scripture and our personal experiences, God miraculously transforms perceived or experienced scarcity into abundance. We will find that "as we continuously make room for God's hospitality, more room will become available for life, hope, and grace."[12] I suggest that the personal experience of this miraculous transformation from scarcity to abundance could be what we perceive as crisis moments in our spiritual journey. It is these moments where we profoundly experience an abundance of grace in such a way that our lives are marked by considerable movement and change.[13] While we will experience crisis moments, most of our journey will consist of smaller steps. Most of our spiritual formation will be gradual, less noticeable movements. However, there will be crisis experiences where we are flooded with an awareness of God's abundant grace. Both these smaller movements and crisis experiences are what constitute discipleship.

How Do We View the Work of the Atonement?

As alluded to earlier, our view of the atonement impacts how we practice discipleship and view God's grace. Some people might suggest that atonement theories are non-essential and need not be considered deeply. Others may say that the work of the atonement is a mystery or covers many theories of atonement. While we can see the merit with some of these suggested points, I suggest that how one conceives of the atonement will greatly impact one's discipleship. I fear that discipleship in American churches has been overly influenced by a penal substitution view of the atonement. Again, my focus here is not to provide an exhaustive work on atonement theories. However, I hope to demonstrate a need to consider thoughtfully what we practically believe about what Christ accomplished through his life, death, and resurrection. I will also demonstrate how a Wesleyan and

---

12. Pohl, *Making*, xiii.
13. Oden, *Welcomed*, 120.

Relational view of salvation finds the penal substitution view deficient in understanding what Christ has accomplished for us.

As we begin to consider how our view of atonement impacts our view of grace, we must ask the question "What end does God have in mind when God gives grace to us?"[14] Is God's only intent in extending grace to us to offer forgiveness or secure a place for us in the after-life? Is it only for God to pretend that God does not see that we are still acting in unloving ways to both God and others? Is grace to be some sort of magical sunglasses so that all God sees is Jesus when God looks at us, while we remain the same deformed, sick people we were before? These are the kind of assumptions the penal substitution theory makes.

Wesley wrestled with this struggle in his day. On one side, he had Calvinism emphasizing God's sovereignty while the Catholic Church was emphasizing human works.[15] Calvin's emphasis on sovereignty created a grace that was irresistible and focused only on forgiveness of sins, while the Catholic position almost removed God acting in grace and placed all effort on the human side or works. Wesley was able to develop a middle way with his concept of prevenient grace. With Wesley's understanding of grace, every human action that was directed toward God was explainable by the prevenient grace of God that acted first, enabling the human response.[16] While Calvinism is focused on pardon only, Wesleyanism holds a dynamic view of grace that emphasizes "pardon and power."[17] It could be said that a Calvinistic view of grace understands grace to be enacted in a "judicial capacity" while a Wesleyan view understands God's grace to be a "healing grace."[18]

For the purpose of this relational discipleship resource, we must work from the premise that God gives grace for the express purpose of empowering a life that is rightly related to God and others.[19] To proceed to engage in discipleship based on a view that God's grace is only to get us off the hook diminishes the optimism of discipleship because this inadequate view of God's grace lacks the full ability and optimism grace truly affords. Because

---

14. Green and Greenway, *Changing*, 97.

15. Crofford, *Streams*, 67.

16. Maddox, *Responsible*, 84. Also see, J. Wesley, "The Principles of a Methodist," *The Works of John Wesley*, vol. 8, 373.

17. Maddox, *Responsible*, 85.

18. Ibid.

19. Green and Greenway, *Changing*, 96.

God's grace is relational, we cannot hold to a view of God's grace where the action is placed solely in some past or future action. Salvation is not limited to only a past or future experience, but God is even now extending grace working to save us now.[20] This ever present grace is relationally engaging us to respond and be transformed even in this moment.

Grace Defined

Grace is one of those words that can be overused and overly simplified so that the impact of the word has little significance when we consider the concept. John Wesley said this about grace, "The grace of God is sometimes to be understood that free love, that unmerited mercy, by which I a sinner through the merits of Christ am now reconciled to God. But in this place, it rather means that power of God the Holy Spirit worketh in us."[21] Wesley would say that grace is "the power of God given through the Holy Spirit, which alone works in us for all that is acceptable to God."[22] We can say that grace is unmerited favor, the many ways God demonstrates God's love toward us, God's enabling action prior to conversion and all the way into sanctification, and "God's loving personal presence in our lives."[23]

We can say that grace is relational because grace is a present initiative of God to invite us "to participate in an ongoing relationship with God."[24] Grace is the "non-coercive influence of God in the world where God lures creation to exhibit beauty."[25] Kenton Stiles says, "Grace is how God enjoys the world."[26] Grace is the way God experiences and interacts in each moment with each of God's creatures.[27] With these views of grace, we can say grace is the initiative and lure in relational discipleship. Further, because we place the initiative and the enabling power with God's grace, Pelagianism

---

20. Knight, *Presence*, 9. Also see, J. Wesley, "Salvation by Faith," *The Works of John Wesley*, vol. 5, 13.

21. Carder and Warner, *Grace*, 11. Also see, J. Wesley, "The Witness of Our Own Spirit," *The Works of John Wesley*, vol. 5, 141.

22. Manskar, *Accountable*, 29.

23. Crofford, *Streams*, 10.

24. Knight, *Presence*, 8.

25. Stone and Oord, *Name*, 283.

26. Ibid.

27. Ibid.

is avoided.[28] We can never boast in human effort. Any human action is a response to prior divine action.[29]

A central component to relational discipleship is the concept of moving home and living in God's house. This living in God's house is analogous to living in an awareness of God's presence. We can suggest this analogy because we can describe God's grace as God's presence.[30] We assert grace as God's presence for several reasons. First, God is love. We have already established that grace is God's loving action toward us. God is also omnipresent because of God's love. God is present to all God's creation in each moment taking the most loving action possible for all of creation. Randy Maddox describes grace as "God's loving personal presence at work in our lives."[31] As we increasingly become aware of God's already at work grace in our lives and increasingly respond in positive ways to that grace, we are, in effect living in God's presence.

In this act of being present in the moment to us, "God condescends to our limited capabilities."[32] In each moment, God is uniquely working with each of us depending where we are in our transformation. God is providing us the light we can handle in each moment. How could we grasp and move toward a God that is wholly other unless God takes on ways we can understand and provides a sense that there is hope of such transformation? God does these very things to enable our self-awareness, to help us recognize the holiness of God, and for us to have the power to move forward in this transformation.[33] God recognizes that we cannot travel the distance from our ways of being to God's wholly other way of being in one short trip. God lovingly walks alongside us, enabling us by grace to move toward holiness. It is in this awareness that we recognize that only God can "heal us of our addiction to sin and our love of comfort over discipleship" and proceed to make the longer and more difficult journey toward transformation.[34]

---

28. Pelagianism can be defined as salvation being accomplished by human will and effort. Wesleyanism has often been accused of being "semi-Pelagianism. Wesley addressed the issue, J. Wesley, *The Works of John Wesley*, vol. 10, 403.

29. Crofford, *Streams*, 190. Also see, J. Wesley, "The Means of Grace," *The Works of John Wesley*, vol. 5, 185.

30. Stone and Oord, *Name*, 99.

31. Maddox, *Responsible*, 86.

32. Ibid., 45.

33. Carder and Warner, *Grace*, 12.

34. Watson, *Class Meeting*, 138.

The Universality and Optimism of Grace

A Wesleyan and Relational view of God's grace is extremely optimistic. Going back to God's economy, this view of grace reveals a God that desires no one to be excluded from God's house and table.[35] We can be confident that God is also actively working toward that end without "coercion."[36] We can be confident that God actively seeks each person.[37] In this assertion, we can say that there is a "measure of grace in every human life" drawing each person to God.[38] God's grace is abundant and universal. The truth is that Jesus suffered and died for each person, and it is God's will that none should be lost (2 Peter 3:9). In our view of God's economy, are we really threatened if this hope were to come true? Is God's grace in scarce supply that we should not also hope and work for what God desires?[39]

This view of grace is also optimistic in that it understands that it is God, who first acts in each moment, enabling us to be aware of God. God's grace acts first enabling us to develop a maturing relationship.[40] In this Wesleyan view, grace has kept humanity from experiencing total depravity. A Wesleyan view admits that our Christ-likeness has been damaged but not totally destroyed. God's prior acting grace ensures that a remnant of God's likeness remains in us which enables us to respond to God.[41] In this view, we are optimistic because we can be confident that God is preceding us wherever and to whomever we go because the divine image remains in every person. God draws us toward God's self because grace interacts with the remaining divine image, awakening us to the things of God.

This optimism of grace compels us to recognize an "infinite variety of God's grace" or action in this world.[42] While the Wesleyan way of salvation typically breaks grace down into prevenient, justifying, and sanctifying grace, God touches every person with grace in as many ways as there are people and moments. God is not constrained to only using certain avenues

---

35. Manskar, *Accountable*, 60.
36. Stone and Oord, *Name*, 99.
37. Reuteler, Heart.
38. Watson, *Covenant*, 37.
39. Watson, *Foreclose*, 13.
40. Blevins and Maddix, *Discovering*, 105.
41. Carder and Warner, *Grace*, 48.
42. Watson, *Foreclose*, 119.

or methods. God's grace is so vast and varied that we can "expect to see it at every turn, in every situation."[43]

The only limit to grace is the limit that is imposed by unbelief.[44] We often limit grace when we believe that sin is greater than grace. We need to fathom the depths of grace as the Holy Spirit leads us to an ever deepening experience of God's love. In this experience, we truly come to terms with God's will. It is God's will that where "sin reigns God's grace will reign instead."[45]

Introduction to Wesley's House of Religion

Wesley used the analogy of a house to depict the Wesleyan way of salvation and the movement through God's grace. We can call it a House of Religion or House of God.[46] Before we engage in an analysis of the metaphor, I want to correct any potential confusion equating the church with being the house of God. There may be some preconceived notions that an actual church building is a house of God or that individual people are the house of God. The first notion takes on an Old Testament view where God inhabits the Temple. The latter takes on a modern view where we ask Jesus into our hearts. While both analogies can have significance, they do not match what Wesley was trying to communicate and what I think much of scripture images for us regarding dwelling in God's presence.

We first must understand that the "Gospel created the church."[47] The Gospel does not belong to the church.[48] In light of this fact, the church is to teach and model grace. The message of the church is grace. The church proclaims and exudes grace in all its forms—prevenient, saving, assuring, perfecting, and glorifying.[49] While the church is not the house of God we will be referencing, "the church is to be a station for God's grace to flow: an aid station where people can find compassion, a saving station where Jesus Christ can be encountered; a filling station where disciples are nurtured; and, a sending station where God's people are sent into mission and

43. Watson, *Foreclose*, 119.
44. Pinnock, *Grace*, 29.
45. Ibid., 80.
46. J. Wesley, *The Works of John Wesley*, vol. 8, 472.
47. Green and Greenway, *Changing*, 52.
48. Ibid.
49. Ibid., 9.

ministry."[50] The church exists to help people on their journey back to God's house or presence.

We often hear the analogy of inviting Jesus into one's heart. This analogy describes God coming into our house. Wesley's approach was instead for us to leave our wandering wilderness and the shacks in which we live and move in with God. He divided the house of religion into three areas of concern. The porch, the door, and the actual rooms of the house were the major components of God's house.[51] The porch represents where a person resides who has been awakened to the things of God. The door is justification. Sanctification is the process of living with God in the actual rooms of the house. The goal is to get people to abandon their "shacks and come in and live and dwell with God."[52]

As we have discussed earlier, God's grace acts first, before people can do anything to respond. In this first action, God's grace goes out from the house in search of lost wrecked lives.[53] God, in the form of grace, goes into humanity leaving the comfort of God's porch seeking the people who cannot find comfort on their own. God watches from the window of God's home for the prodigal to return. When God sees one walking afar off, God jumps up and sets out to the one God sees. God's grace goes and helps the person have an awareness that God's house is there for refuge. God's prevenient grace invites the traveler to the porch of religion.

People gather on the porch of religion to get to know the neighbor who has invited them over. They learn much about the neighbor by the hospitality and grace offered to them while they visit on the porch. People discover that they have been seeking this neighbor as a friend because this neighbor is "close and available."[54] What these people have yet to recognize is that "even as they ever so slightly begin to let their guard down and respond to this grace, redemption has begun."[55] These people sitting on the porch think God is just being neighborly and friendly. What they do not realize yet, is that God is their long lost Father desiring to reconnect with his children. We can call this grace convincing grace. The porch is where God is convincing people that they need God.

50. Green and Greenway, *Changing*, 3.
51. Watson, *Blueprint*, 33. Also see, J. Wesley, *The Works of John Wesley*, vol. 8, 472.
52. Watson, *Blueprint*, 34. Also see, J. Wesley, *The Works of John Wesley*, vol. 8, 373.
53. Reuteler, *Heart*.
54. Lodahl, *Nature*, 115.
55. Ibid., 140.

As God sees people responding to the grace God has offered, God will extend the next invitation. God asks, "Won't you come into my house and visit?" God will encourage people to walk through the door, but God will not force God's hospitality onto others. The person may not be quite settled and comfortable in accepting the graciousness of God. God allows the person to remain on the porch and continues to pour out as much grace as God can on the porch. Unfortunately, some people will leave the porch because of decisions and distractions. However, God's grace will still be inviting those people back to the porch of God.

The people that accept God's invitation walk through the door of justification. These people have heard the story of God on the porch. They heard how the Son died for the people of the world. Yet, as they walk through the door of justification, they discover that Jesus died specifically for them.[56] They become aware that they are children of this God who invited them in. They see portraits of them being a child of God hanging on the wall across the room. From the door of justification, they recognize their broken relationship with Dad is being healed. Sins are forgiven. They are reclaiming their position as sons and daughters of this loving Father. This home was meant to be theirs all along.

Wesley indicated that many people stopped either at the porch of religion or the door of religion.[57] It did not make sense to Wesley how people could experience the grace of God and not want to move from the porch or door of religion. In fact, in reality people can and will leave the door and porch to go back to their old shacks of life. Wesley felt that Methodism was particularly called for the express purpose of helping people move from the porch and door of religion into the whole house of God being sanctification.[58]

As people become aware of their place as children of God, God offers the next invitation of grace, the grace to return home or sanctifying grace. God desires that the children move back home with God and live with God. This moving back home brings the child and Father back into a right relationship. They can love as they were created to love. God does not want us to live part time with God and part time in our wrecked shacks of

---

56. Watson, *Blueprint*, 18.
57. Ibid., 35.
58. J. Wesley, *The Works of John Wesley*, vol. 8, 299.

life.[59] God does not want shared visitation rights. God does not want only weekend visits.

As we live with God, we then can love others properly as well. We cannot love rightly apart from an ongoing relationship with God. We also cannot grow in love apart from getting to know God better.[60] Sanctification can be seen as "exploring the rooms of God's house."[61] We can explore different qualities of God's holiness by moving from room to room. God's house is amazingly big with multiple possibilities for exploration and discovery. Gregory Clapper adds that when our behaviors can be traced back to perfect love we have arrived at sanctification.[62] God is always inviting to the next place in God's house. The response to God's invitation is ours to accept or reject. Will we go all the way with God and return to God's house and live with God? Will we move all of our lives completely into God's house?[63] This moving back home with God is relational discipleship.

God's Grace is Never Coercive or Irresistible

We have established that God's grace enables and empowers us to respond to God. Without God's grace we cannot be saved, however "without our participation God will not save."[64] God will not impose God's grace upon us irresistibly.[65] Because the goal of grace is relationship, it cannot be forced or irresistible.[66] God is a God of "impeccable manners."[67] God will lure with the beauty of God's holiness or perfect love, but God will never coerce or force subjugation.[68] We must cooperate in each moment with God's loving invitation to draw closer in God's presence.

---

59. Reuteler, *Heart*.
60. Knight, *Presence*, 10.
61. Clapper, *Heart*, 87.
62. Ibid., 71.
63. Watson, *Class Meeting*, 46.
64. Watson, *Blueprint*, 30.
65. Rakestraw, *Wesley*, 198.
66. Knight, *Presence*, 9.
67. Watson, *Covenant*, 109.
68. Oord, *Love*, 148.

Our Response to God's Grace

As we have established, God's grace is neither coercive nor irresistible. The nature of God's grace enables and empowers free will and the ability to respond to God's grace. I have indicated previously that all grace is the same. However, our response creates "theological distinctions" in how that grace is appropriated to us and how we experience God's grace.[69] The continued task of discipleship is to help us cooperate with God's grace.[70] Simplified further, responding positively to grace could be described as learning to say "yes" to God.[71] Discipleship can be best described as an ongoing response to grace and not just instant transformation.[72]

If a person desires to have more grace in her life, then the most assured way is to use and "appropriate the grace" God is currently extending to the person.[73] Because God never imposes grace, God cannot extend more grace to a person than that person is willing to use and appropriate. This appropriation of grace could be described much like breathing. God is always present and we at times take God's grace for granted as we do the air we breathe.[74] However, as we grow in awareness and responsive to God's grace, we will experience greater degrees of grace. In this awareness, we learn that we do not need to sin as long as we remain responsive to God's grace.[75]

This process of responding to God's grace leads to a mutual cooperation that we can describe as hospitality. We learn that we are friends with God and build upon that friendship as we cooperate with God's grace.[76] This hospitality is fostered as we listen to grace and allow grace to flow through us to others.[77] In the next chapter, we will find that this cooperation is experienced by the means of grace. In the other two models of discipleship that are prevalent in today's church, means of grace are either practiced to increase one's knowledge of truth and doctrine or engaged

---

69. Lodahl, *Nature*, 140.
70. Watson, *Covenant*, 37.
71. Ibid.
72. Stone and Oord, *Name*, 73.
73. Rakestraw, *Wesley*, 202.
74. Manskar, Suchocki, and Hynson, *Understanding*, 140.
75. Maddox, *Responsible*, 164.
76. Carder and Warner, *Grace*, 11.
77. Boren, *Relational*, 124.

to better one's self and satisfaction. In relational discipleship, the means of grace are a means to experiencing both God and others in a way that mutually communicate and experience grace. We will find that opening ourselves up to God and other people's hospitality, and in turn, extending hospitality to God and others is the vehicle through which we communicate and experience God's grace.

3

Hospitality—
Grace Expressed, Received, and Shared

The Aroma of Hospitality

Think back to a special place that you fondly remember. This particular place is one where you walked in and felt at home, especially a place where you felt at home as soon as you smelled some of your favorite foods. Maybe this memory is grandma's place on Thanksgiving Day, or maybe this memory takes you back home to mom and dad's place for Christmas. Do you have a place in mind? What was the aroma that flooded your senses as you walked through the door? Was it the turkey? The ham? Was it the apple pie fresh out of the oven? The bread baking? Your favorite cake? I am not a coffee drinker, but sometimes the aroma of coffee has that effect on me. Our minds are funny by the way certain aromas can trigger a fond memory that we have of home.

Have you located that memory? Are you going back to that time where you felt at home as soon as you walked through the door and enjoyed the aroma that was flooding your senses? Maybe the sense of smell was so strong you can almost taste the food right now: but more importantly, you have memories of people who created a sense of home. These people showed you hospitality.

Consider the story we find in Genesis 18 of Abraham and Sarah's view and practice of hospitality. We first must understand that Abraham and Sarah were nomadic people. They traveled place to place as they headed toward the home to which God had called them. As nomads, they lived in

Hospitality—Grace Expressed, Received, and Shared

a tent. Please keep the word "tent" in the back of your mind. Soon we will see the word "tent" used again.

The first thing we notice about Abraham in Genesis 18 is that he has a spirit of hospitality. In Abraham's day and his culture, hospitality was essential in caring for each other. Hospitality was literally a matter of life and death. Travel was difficult. Resources were at times very hard to come by. People depended on each other to be hospitable. In fact, hospitality was of such great importance in this culture that Ezekiel said the real sin of Sodom and Gomorrah was their lack of hospitality (Ezek. 16:49).

Abraham took hospitality seriously to the extent that he was always on the lookout for travelers. He would watch the road from his tent's entrance. He was looking for and ready to greet and help any traveler that came along. On this particular day, Abraham spotted three travelers from his tent's entrance. We find Abraham running toward and bowing before these travelers. We are told this happened at the hottest time of the day when people were normally asleep.

Not only did he have a desire to show hospitality, but he also did not judge the qualifications of the travelers. At this point in the story, Abraham does not know this is God and God's party traveling. He did not know if these travelers were sinners, attackers, thieves, friendly, wealthy, poor, or idol worshippers. Abraham did not judge these travelers. Additionally, Abraham assigned to these travelers unsurpassable worth by bowing in respect and eagerly greeting these unknown strangers.

Abraham could have ignored these travelers. He could have said, "I do not know what kind of people they are. Maybe they will attack my people; ruin my belongings; steal my belongings; corrupt my people; or share their ungodly ways. Look at their clothes! Oh, how they will smell from traveling in the hot sun." Abraham could have said, "It is just too hot to bother. They will be fine. Let them go on their way." No, Abraham, without casting any judgment, ran toward these strangers and bowed before them. Abraham had a heart after God. Abraham demonstrated hospitality the same way God does.

Abraham then offers his resources to the unknown strangers. For instance, water was a scarce commodity. Abraham offers them water to wash their feet. Abraham did not have lemonade to offer, but he offered cool water and a shade tree to these strangers. He then offered to feed them. Abraham wanted people, he did not even know, to stick around and have a meal with him. Is Abraham a lunatic? Today, we might say that we live in dangerous times and that we could never do that. However, these were dangerous times as well.

Abraham is so hospitable that he hurried again to Sarah and told her to make some bread and other baked goods quickly. Can you imagine the aroma these strangers were beginning to smell? There is nothing like fresh, hot bread baking.

I am beginning to think Abraham did not do anything slowly. We are now told that Abraham ran to the cattle. He picked the best of the herd and asked his servant to prepare the calf as fast as the servant could. Can you imagine the barbecue the strangers were beginning to smell? The smoke from the fire? The smell of beef being flame broiled? If you could smell hospitality, this would be it; the bread baking and the young calf roasting. Can you smell it as the strangers do?

To top it all off, Abraham still did not know who these people were. Even more, Abraham acted with great intensity and speed. He did not want his guests to wait. He knew they were hungry, tired, exhausted, and needed rest and refreshment. Abraham felt honored to entertain potential sinners, thieves, attackers, idolaters, or even angels of God. He was quick to serve them regardless of whom they may have been. He did not judge them. He was not concerned if they smelled, were rich or poor, dangerous, or sinners. He didn't care how they dressed or looked. He didn't think twice how they might break his favorite chair or dirty his best table cloth. He had a heart after God, to extend God's gracious call to hospitality.

We have the benefit of knowing the whole story. We read how it was God and his party traveling through the land. But, what do you think those travelers were thinking, sensing, smelling, seeing, and experiencing as Abraham's guests? People can smell hospitality. It may be in tangible ways like smelling bread baking and the roast simmering. They also smell hospitality, or the lack of it, in less tangible ways. These strangers smelled hospitality when Abraham ran to them, did not judge them, and bowed. They sensed authentic hospitality when they watched Abraham's haste to get a meal ready. Deep hospitality was found in offering a cup of cold water. They smelled Abraham's hospitality.

I want to leave you with a thought as we move forward from Abraham's example of hospitality. Just like you smelled the baking pie or roasting turkey, or whatever you remembered at the beginning of this chapter, people can smell hospitality coming from us. We either exude the aroma of hospitality or inhospitality.

Hospitality—Grace Expressed, Received, and Shared

We display a lack of hospitality when we ignore people while we walk by them without acknowledging them, when we decide not to eat at the same table with people, when we act judgmentally, or when we decide their sin requires us to shun them. People sense our lack of hospitality when we are afraid to interact with others and be involved in their lives beyond Sunday morning. Lack of hospitality is deeply experienced when we do not listen to another person's story. People can smell these actions. It exudes the aroma of being inhospitable. People know to avoid those who stink of inhospitality. Why would they risk approaching someone who sends signals of disdain for people like them?

The same is true of people who bear the aroma of hospitality. I submit to you that Jesus was hospitable, as was Abraham. Jesus did not care if someone was a prostitute, adulterer, tax collector, drunk, Pharisee, rich, poor, or even demon possessed. The crowds smelled Jesus' hospitality and flocked to Him. We have to ask ourselves, what are people smelling from us? Do we stink with inhospitality? Or do they smell the sweet aroma of God's gracious call to hospitality?

Another hospitality passage, Psalm 15, begins with a question posed to God. The question is "Who can live in your tent, Lord? Who can dwell on your holy mountain?" These are important questions to be asked of God. In this Psalm, we find God's response to who can live with God.

I have been positing that there is a theme throughout scripture that God has always been creating home for us and inviting us to return home to God. We find this same theme in Psalm 15. There are two different concepts about living in God's presence here. One is a familiar living with God in the mundane as in living in God's tent. The other is to recognize the awe and otherness of God in the Holy Mountain.

The analogy in Psalm 15 reveals that God has desired to be close to us, so God has moved in, up the hill from us, on the mountain. God does not desire a mere acknowledgment that we believe in Jesus and have recognized that we are sinners at some point in time in the past. God wants us to live with God, in God's house, or *tent*, each and every day, each and every moment—to continually be in God's presence.

What is interesting is that the Hebrew word for "live" in verse one is the word *guwr*. This word better translates as "sojourn," or, "to live as aliens."[1] "Live" in this verse implies that, just like the travelers who depended on Abraham's hospitality, we come to God's tent as aliens and are dependent

---

1. "Hebrew Lexicon: H1481 (NIV)." Blue Letter Bible.

on God's hospitality. Just as Abraham offered God hospitality, God offers us hospitality. We are strangers and travelers, who are wounded and tired on this journey of life. We are very much dependent on God's hospitality.

What is God's answer for what it takes to live continually with God in God's house? If we take scripture seriously, then we will hear what God's answer is in the following verses. In these following verses, we find God communicating a deep value for hospitality. We cannot continue to live in God's presence without demonstrating the same hospitality God extends to us. For instance, to live blameless and do what is right (v.2) is not so much referring to keeping a list of "do's and don'ts" as it is referring to the quality of relationships we have with others. Unfortunately, we have often reduced blameless, righteousness, and holiness to a list of legalistic requirements. I propose to you that legalism is the easy way out. If you study the Hebrew words for blameless and right, you will see it goes much further and deeper than some legalistic checklist.

We see throughout the Old Testament how Israel thought they were right and blameless by doing the correct sacrifices and offerings. They were checking off the boxes to their version of religion. We see in scripture where God says God is tired of these external religious acts, and God doesn't want another offering (Isaiah 1:11 and Hosea 6:6). What God wants is for God's people to live in right relationship with God and others—to offer God's gracious example of hospitality. Micah 6:8 says, "He has shown you, O mortal, what is good. And what does the Lord require of you? To act justly and to love mercy and to walk humbly with your God." This verse describes the type of right and blameless living God desires.

Churches have often taken the easy path of legalism. I am not saying that there are not proper ways to live, but when we focus on our checklists we sacrifice that which is of greater importance to God—hospitality. We miss the mark. Hospitality always has precedence over our checklists of right and wrong.

This Psalm further adds, "Who does no damage with their talk" (v.3). This statement covers a lot of ground. We can hurt others with our mouths and by our words exclude others from hospitality. This verse further adds, "The person who does no harm to a friend" and "doesn't insult a neighbor." These statements express further examples of what hospitality looks like. The next verse states, "despising those who act wickedly" (v.4). Because I want to address verse four more deeply, I will come back to it in a moment. I am sure we have some preconceived ideas about what that means.

Psalm 15 goes on to tell us that we live in God's presence when we keep our promises even when it hurts; when we will not take advantage of people in need; and when we will not lie against an innocent person (v.5). All of these concepts relate directly to how we smell of hospitality. In fact, later in this chapter, I will demonstrate how much of Psalm 15 translates into "key traits of hospitality." God takes hospitality very seriously. It is not reserved for someone who thinks they have a gift of hospitality. We are all called to be hospitable as we live in God's presence.

Just as the strangers were smelling the hospitality coming from Abraham in the bread baking, beef roasting, the cold glass of water, and in the urgency with which Abraham carried out these acts, so too, God's house must smell this same way. This fact is why it is impossible to live in God's presence and not be hospitable. God does not want someone polluting God's place with the stench of being inhospitable. If we truly desire to live in God's presence daily, we will do so to the extent that we are willing and anxious to practice indiscriminate biblical hospitality.

Now, I would like to consider how verse 4 discusses the idea of despising those who act wickedly. Jesus describes what acting wickedly looks like in Matthew 25:31-46. In this passage, Jesus demonstrates just how important hospitality is and who are righteous and who are the wicked. We have Jesus expressing that those who are hospitable—who feed the hungry, give a drink to those that are thirsty, welcome the stranger, give clothing to others, and visit the sick and imprisoned are the ones who receive the ultimate opportunity of eternally living in God's presence. Conversely, we see who the wicked are that are referenced in Psalm 15. They are ones who refused to offer God's gracious call to hospitality. They would not have fed the travelers as Abraham did. They would not have offered a glass of water to Abraham's visitors. Unlike Abraham, they would not have welcomed the strangers.

Both the hospitable and inhospitable people asked Jesus to provide an example of when they had encountered Him as a thirsty and hungry stranger. Jesus indicated for every time they did it to the least of Jesus' brothers and sisters, they did it to Jesus Himself. Jesus was already there. Abraham was a perfect example of this. He did not know that God was in the midst of the traveling strangers, but Abraham soon found out that he was hospitable to God.

Our understanding of hospitality reflects what we really believe about God's grace and love. If we truly believe that God is omnipresent—that

God is everywhere—then we recognize that God is already present with the stranger, our enemy, the sick, the hungry, the wounded, and the sinner. If we truly believe that God's grace is prevenient—meaning always going before; and, if we believe that grace is universal—meaning that grace is active and alive in everyone, then we will truly act in a hospitable manner to all we encounter.

It is easy to say we love our enemies and to say we love others. It is even easy to throw money at a problem or a person. While those things are important, scripture indicates that laying down our lives demonstrates love (1 John 3:16). However, the first way we demonstrate love is by recognizing or acknowledging the person.[2] Being hospitable is first recognizing and acknowledging a person's unsurpassable worth. Additionally, we must recognize that God is already present to the person whether the person or we readily recognize God already at work (Matthew 25:40).

We are hospitable to someone when we greet her. We are inhospitable when we ignore the person. We are hospitable to someone when we take the time to hear her story; what is bothering her and troubling her. We are inhospitable when we do not truly listen to a person. We are hospitable and reinforce someone's worth when we sit down and eat with the person. We are inhospitable when we refuse to eat with that person. Hospitality is a grace that God extends to us continually. God is continually offering a gracious call through God's hospitality to live in God's presence. At the same time, we can offer acts of grace to others that affirm the unsurpassable worth of the other person thereby extending God's hospitality through us.

We must ask ourselves, what is our aroma? Do we stink with inhospitality? Or, do people sense God's hospitality within us? This true hospitality can only happen as we experience and accept God's welcome. We are told in 1 John 4:19 that we love because God first loved us. We cannot offer hospitality to others and God until we embrace the hospitality God offers us.

In the relational discipleship model, it is not sufficient to only want to change or transform the disciple. The discipler, must in fact, be transformed first in order to extend biblical hospitality to the disciple. This resource embraces the reality that the state of the discipler is equally as important, or perhaps even more important, than the practical steps to be taken to disciple another person. Before relational discipleship can begin with a disciple, the discipler must experience the relational components

---

2. Boyd, *Repenting*, 30.

being addressed. Before a discipler can disciple someone, the discipler must experience and exhibit biblical hospitality.

People Are Hungry for Hospitality

I suggest that the withholding of hospitality and the abuse of hospitality are what makes a mess of God's home. The withholding of hospitality and the abuse of hospitality are results of our original sin.[3] When we judge others, we withhold hospitality and the resources that enable others to flourish. We judge others as being somehow unworthy of our hospitality. We may even judge that certain people will take advantage of our hospitality. Conversely, when we judge that others may threaten our ability to flourish, we may then begin to abuse or take advantage of the hospitality others extend to us. We may cheat, lie, or steal from others in order to take advantage of their resources. Both actions originate from judging others.

Howard Snyder describes this judgment as predation.[4] To go a step further, Snyder describes sinful actions as predatory.[5] We prey on people when we are willing to sacrifice others for our benefit.[6] On the other hand, Jesus' way displays a wholly other way of being—that of self-emptying love. This may be what Jesus was talking about when he told us to pick up our cross, deny ourselves, and follow Him (Matthew 16:24–26). We have a choice to be either a predator or a follower of Christ. Predators either withhold hospitality or take advantage of others who offer hospitality by being willing to sacrifice other's ability to flourish for the sake of the predator. To follow Christ is to offer hospitality even in the face of rejection or in being taken advantage of by placing importance on the other's ability to flourish. We call this self-denial or the act of self-emptying love.

Let us consider the abuse of hospitality that Jesus took in laying down his life for us. He did not demand protection of the hospitality he offered in his life and death. He freely gave from his self-emptying love, even to those who abused, rejected, and took advantage of his hospitality. We, in the same way, are asked to take up our crosses and deny ourselves. This self-denial includes not withholding hospitality from people we deem undeserving.

---

3. Pohl, *Making*, 21.
4. Snyder, *Salvation Means Creation Healed*, 101.
5. Ibid.
6. Ibid.

Often, many people assume that they must protect themselves and the church from people who would abuse and take advantage of hospitality. While there is some level of concern, it is impossible for us to judge properly and fairly those who are abusing hospitality. In this current world, there should be a measure of safeguarding against abuse of hospitality. However, I would suggest that threshold should be very low. Those who are abusing hospitality can experience healing as we do not judge them by causing them to feel threatened more by withholding hospitality. Withholding hospitality will only increase the perceived threat they feel to their ability to flourish and will only serve to increase their abuse of hospitality. The church is to be communicating the abundance of God's grace, and not creating a sense of scarcity by overly protecting against abuse.[7]

We need to begin to see people as they really are: those in need of grace. These people are virtual prisoners of war—not the enemy we think they are. We need to see people with the eyes of Christ: sick, hungry, a stranger, or a traveler. Every person in the world is hungry for abundant life, but many times are passed by while the church hoards its grace in "bigger barns" (Luke 12:13–21).[8] The people of the world press their noses against the windows of these barns not knowing how to get in.[9] People believe they are not welcome because they perceive Christians to be hostile toward them as they sense the aroma of inhospitality from many Christians. The church often fails to make the welcome and hospitality of God "plain and easily grasped."[10]

Restoring authentic hospitality is essential in allowing the kingdom of God to come now into our world. Authentic hospitality is an essential aspect of relational discipleship, where people can feel safe at home which promotes and allows for real transformation. Authentic, biblical hospitality creates a feeling of home and enters into the very presence of God because it is the extending, receiving, and sharing the active grace of God.

Disciplers using a relational discipleship model will view each person as hungry for abundant life and deserving of biblical hospitality. Only as this view becomes the way we orient our lives and our discipleship, will people feel safe to move toward God's house. As people perceive this hospitality, people will be drawn to at least visit the porch of God. Only when

---

7. I address extensively God's economy of abundance in chapter two on grace.
8. Oden, *Gospel*, 27.
9. Ibid.
10. Ibid.

people feel the warmth of hospitality will they feel safe enough to let their guard down. In the safety of hospitality, they can confess where they have traveled from on this journey to God's house.

God's Hospitality

We can assert that God extends hospitality first as I have described God's grace as always prevenient—always preceding and acting first. Earlier, we examined the Trinity. The very interaction of the three persons of the Trinity establishes hospitality. Hospitality begins when the Trinity invites us into interaction with God. God takes the initiative by being hospitable toward us.[11] Jesus' incarnation further demonstrates God's hospitable initiative.[12] Additionally, God's holiness can be equated to God offering hospitality first. The holiness of God is so supremely other that God acts first to offer "supreme mercy, longsuffering, everlasting love, and a desire for universal inclusiveness."[13]

This initiative in extending hospitality is always an invitation for every person to come home to God, or, to put it differently, to move closer to God in each moment. This invitation is always "universal and meant for all."[14] In this universal invitation, we find that the religious have often been annoyed by God's invitation. God's guest list emphasizes the marginalized, stranger, and wounded people. In Jesus' time, Jesus' guest list irritated those people who thought they were on the "preferred guest list."[15]

God's welcome has some recurring themes and traits. One theme is that God's welcome occurs repeatedly.[16] There is never a moment where God is not welcoming and inviting each of us one step closer to God and in God. A trait we see is that God's invitation is a personal invitation to the table.[17] God enjoys fellowshipping and celebrating with God's family. Because God is near, God's welcome is as "close as our breath."[18] This trait demonstrates that we do not have to "look for God's invitation, wait for

---

11. Oden, *Welcomed*, 108.
12. Ibid., 110.
13. Stone and Oord, *Name*, 80.
14. Pohl, *Making*, 21.
15. Ibid., 17.
16. Oden, *Gospel*, 32.
17. Ibid., 33.
18. Ibid.

God's invitation, or earn God's invitation." God's welcome is not partial, tentative, or conditional.[19] We have already established that God's welcome reveals miraculous abundance.[20] Finally, we experience God's welcome as we experience God's grace luring us to move deeper in God's presence.[21] These themes demonstrate the depth and width of God's hospitality.

Jesus' invitations in the gospels reveal the same degrees of faith and grace that John Wesley describes.[22] The first invitation Jesus offered was to "come and see" (John 1:39—4:46). Jesus was extending prevenient grace and hospitality to people by asking them just to come and see who he was and what he was up to. The next invitation Jesus offered was to "come and follow me" (Matthew 4:19). The third invitation was "come and be with me" (Mark 3:13-14). We can associate these invitations to Wesley's convincing and justifying graces, where Jesus wants people to identify with Him and become like Him. Finally, Jesus offered the invitation to "remain in me" (John 15:1-17). Again, we can see the suggestion of living in God's presence, or as Wesley said, God's house. We can associate remaining in God with sanctifying grace.[23]

We Accept and Extend God's Hospitality— Holiness of Heart and Life

The church has been prone to view holiness from a legalistic perspective, where God has been seen to have arbitrarily decided what God likes and dislikes.[24] This restrictive view of God's grace then translates into a list of do's and don'ts that Christians follow in order to be holy. While in reality, holiness is nothing less than perfect love.[25] God is holy because God's way of being is so different than ours. To say it differently, God's way of loving is so different than ours. We complicate holiness and perfect love when we attempt to qualify further God's love as "holy love." In this attempt, we are being redundant

19. Oden, *Gospel*, 34.
20. Ibid., 37.
21. Ibid., 38.
22. Hull, *Complete*, 164. Also see, J. Wesley, "The Scripture Way of Salvation," *The Works of John Wesley*, vol. 6, 508.
23. J. Wesley, "The Means of Grace," *The Works of John Wesley*, vol. 5, 185.
24. Thomas Oord wrestles with this concept. Oord, *Uncontrolling*, 46.
25. J. Wesley, "A Plain Account of Christian Perfection," *The Works of John Wesley*, vol. 11, 383.

and cause further misunderstanding of the terms holy and love.[26] We create a sense that to be holy is somehow different than acting in loving ways. The terms holy and holiness is simply perfect love expressed and experienced.[27] What is right and wrong in God's eyes is determined by perfect love.

The church has often withheld hospitality because it wants to preserve a false notion of holiness. As a result of not understanding the true notion of holiness as perfect love, the church has often deemed holiness as fragile and easily contaminated. In reality, holiness is accepting and extending God's hospitality without reservation. Holiness is not "distancing ourselves from the world but rather being engaged in the world."[28] Again, all we need to do is look at God, who is holy. God is fully engaged in the world. Jesus even went to the extent of becoming human.

The church further misses the mark with holiness when the church overly protects a notion of cleanliness. At times, the church fears that its holiness will be soiled. When we make this assumption, we fail to recognize "that in order to get clean often something has to get dirty."[29] When we take a bath, the bathtub gets dirty. A health care professional often gets dirty to help heal a person. A parent will get dirty in saving a child who fell in the mud. Jesus got dirty by becoming fully human and taking on our sins and violence on the cross. Jesus' holiness shined even brighter and clearer as he was willing to engage and get dirty to clean, heal, and save the world. Holiness is not afraid to get dirty in extending hospitality.

We only gain the confidence to extend hospitality in these situations by first experiencing the welcome God extends. When we have the assurance that we are loved, we have "the confidence and freedom to love others."[30] This kind of hospitality is possible as we become aware of God's continued presence in our lives, even in the ordinary and mundane.[31] As we make room for God and others in our hearts, hospitality becomes a reality.[32] Once we realize that we are offering God's welcome, we are freed to offer this hospitality without reservation.[33] It is when we assume that it is our

---

26. Oord, *Love*, 8.
27. Wynkoop, *Theology*, 115
28. Stone and Oord, *Name*, 80.
29. Ibid.
30. Stone and Oord, *Name*, 81.
31. Oden, *Welcomed*, xiii.
32. Pohl, *Making*, 152.
33. Oden, *Gospel*, 12.

welcome that we begin to make judgments about who is deserving or not deserving of this welcome and offer to abundant life. Finally, we imitate the welcome and hospitality we see God offer.[34] As we see God's willingness to extend mercy, forgiveness, life, and love to people who do not deserve it (including ourselves), we can in turn offer that indiscriminate hospitality.

All Hospitality is Done to Jesus

We are reminded in Matthew 25 that all hospitality done to the "least of these" is done to Jesus. Jesus is already present and active in people to whom we extend hospitality.[35] Therefore, every action of hospitality or refusal of hospitality is being done to Jesus. Jesus experiences what we do to others.[36] If we take what Jesus said in Matthew 25 seriously, then we understand that when we extend hospitality to others we are in a very real sense becoming the guest of God.[37] When we take Jesus seriously, we recognize that God has already been present and at work in the people we offer hospitality to before we even arrive.[38] However, we must accept that God may not be working on that person in the ways that we expect. We may think a particular sin or disposition needs to be worked on first. We must accept how God is currently working in the person's life at this moment. In fact, we should not be offering hospitality to anyone with changing or fixing a person as our goal. Hospitality should be offered indiscriminately.

A Working Definition

Hospitality is a multi-faceted array of activities and dispositions. To take hospitality back to its earliest of intentions, we must see what God intended hospitality to look like. If we look at God's original intent for creation, hospitality occurs when people open themselves up to God's life and revelation.[39] In this opening ourselves up to God's life and revelation, we find God to be the source of abundant life. God intended and intends for creation to flourish.

---

34. Oden, *Welcomed*, 88.
35. Heuertz and Pohl, *Friendship*, 19.
36. Ibid., 10.
37. Oden, *Welcomed*, 51.
38. Pohl, *Making*, 68.
39. Oden, *Welcomed*, 15.

When people are rightly related to God and others, then people experience this source of life and find God revealing God to them.

Hospitality is the central way God builds and maintains God's household.[40] We help God's home (kingdom) flourish in the here and now when we extend hospitality. As I mentioned, hospitality includes a wide array of activities. We will now move on to explore some of the essential activities and qualities that exist in being hospitable. When we are hospitable, we are concerned about basic necessities of life being met.[41] Food, clothing, water, shelter, and inclusion are what people need to survive. As this hospitality is extended, both the guest and host will experience joy, pain, crisis, and peace.[42] The process of hospitality will often feel like a rollercoaster matching the ups and downs of life. To engage in hospitality will cost time, resources, space, and love. Offering God's welcome will mean that we value people differently than the way the world values people.[43] To value people differently is what it means for a Christian to be counter-cultural to the world. Hospitality is the vehicle through which God and people express, receive, and share grace.

In relational discipleship, the discipler is not solely interested in the spiritual transformation or the transfer of right doctrines to a disciple. The discipler is first and foremost valuing the disciple as a person who possesses the unsurpassable worth that God intends to flourish with abundant life. The discipler is concerned with hospitality that addresses the whole person and the ability of that person to flourish here and now. The means of grace become the way in which we experience and share this hospitality. Only when the disciple experiences this level of hospitality will the disciple be able to experience both spiritual transformation and a renewed ability to flourish in this life.[44]

Who is Invited?

Relational discipleship has a direct concern for the marginalized and those without a voice. These people are vulnerable, easily ignored, and do not

---

40. Meeks, *Economist*, 88.
41. Ibid., 94.
42. Pohl, *Making*, 10.
43. Pohl, *Making*, 61.
44. Ibid., x.

bring status or financial gain to the people who reach out to them.[45] In fact, these people may bring condemnation on us from others, including church people, when we offer hospitality to them because these groups are not valuing these people with God's way of valuing. There is nothing to gain in reaching out to these people except the gift of who the person is and who is already present with them—Jesus Christ. These guests cannot repay and, therefore, are often judged as unworthy of hospitality.

Luke 14:13–23 lists the people we are told to invite back home. The lame, the poor, the crippled, and blind are to receive the first and priority invite. These people are strange and therefore strangers to us and often make us uncomfortable by their strangeness. As strangers, they are often disconnected from those that can help them because of their strangeness. As a result, they are not able to flourish.[46] The strangers that Jesus indicated as the ones to be invited to the banquet may not be physically blind, crippled, lame, or poor, but these same wounds could be spiritual or social in nature. We see these people as different to us because we find little in common with them.[47] Their particular sins are too different from ours. Their lifestyles and ways of interacting with others are a world apart from ours. We often withhold hospitality from these different people because we judge their perceived strangeness to us. Yet, we find exhortations throughout scripture to love and to be hospitable to the stranger (Leviticus 19:34, Deuteronomy 10:19, and Hebrews 13:1).

Leviticus 19:34 "You shall treat the stranger who sojourns with you as the native among you, and you shall love him as yourself, for you were strangers in the land of Egypt: I am the Lord your God" (ESV).

What Hospitality Looks Like

As I mentioned earlier, hospitality takes on a wide array of activities and disposition. We see Jesus offering hospitality in many forms throughout his life. The early church also demonstrates hospitality in various forms. Scriptures show activities like: foot washing (bathing and hygiene), healing (medical treatment), shelter, clothing, supplies for the journey, care of animals, mentoring, visiting, and one that often offers the most welcome—eating a

---

45. Oden, *Welcomed*, 20.
46. Pohl, *Making*, 13.
47. Ibid., 86.

meal with a person.[48] We could list many more examples of hospitality, but I would like to focus on the sharing of a meal.

There is a big difference between serving a hungry or poor person a meal and actually eating with this person. In eating with a person, we are acknowledging her worth, being present to the person, indicating we are on the same level, and expressing our enjoyment of the person's presence. Scripture communicates time and again that Jesus ate with people, including sinners and tax collectors. He was ascribing unsurpassable worth to people whom the religious people of the day were describing as unworthy. He refused to accept the religious valuing system and instead maintained his Father's view of humanity.

Another important form that hospitality takes involves suffering with the person.[49] As I previously mentioned, hospitality will often feel like a rollercoaster. Hospitality will match the highs and lows of life as we make ourselves available to others. When we are truly available for someone, we will suffer and share the pain he or she feels and experiences. We will attempt to view life from the person's perspective. Putting ourselves into her shoes will cause us to feel and experience what she is enduring.[50]

Key Traits of Hospitality[51]

In the discussion of Psalm 15, I alluded to the fact that hospitality also involves a disposition. A wrong spirit or attitude will cause us to be inhospitable. This inhospitable spirit includes grumbling, resentment, pride, and arrogance.[52] We can almost match a hospitable spirit or disposition to the fruits of the Spirit that Paul lists (Galatians 5:22–23). A hospitable disposition will include: "humility, gratitude, mercy, compassion, eagerness, liberality, and a willingness to take risks."[53] In the remainder of this chapter, we will look at key traits of hospitality and the cycle and stages of hospitality that will help us move toward a disposition of hospitality.

Gratitude and celebration are key traits of hospitality. Instead of expecting the guest to show gratitude for the host's welcome, the biblically

48. Oden, *Welcomed*, 14.
49. Ibid., 109.
50. Pohl, *Making*, 65.
51. Pohl, *Living*, 11.
52. Oden, *Welcomed*, 101.
53. Ibid., 100.

hospitable host will express genuine gratitude for the opportunity to serve and welcome the guest.[54] The host demonstrates this gratitude by celebrating the guest's arrival.[55] We do not express gratitude and celebrate as a means to change the guest, but we do recognize the impact it has on both the guest and host. Acknowledgment of a person demonstrates the person's value and welcome.

Gratitude is the appropriate response to hospitality and grace.[56] We can offer genuine gratitude to the guests we encounter when we have gratitude for the hospitality God and others have given us.[57] This gratitude begins as we pay attention to the hospitality God and others are extending to us in our lives.[58] This recognition takes place at worship services, the Eucharist, shared meals, parties, and the life events of others.[59] By taking the time to be aware and grateful for the hospitality of God and others, we bring to life our own extension of hospitality toward others and increase our gratitude for the guest.

Friendship is another key trait of hospitality. Friendship is displayed by how we welcome others, the interest we show in them, and the time we devote to them.[60] In friendship, we see the guest not as an object to change but as a fellow traveler.[61] Friendship requires a deep relationship, mutual appreciation, and communion.[62] Biblical hospitality will require friendship that crosses divisions of class, education, race, gender, ethnicity, age, ability, lifestyles, and sins.[63]

We see in God, the ability and desire to make friends of enemies. John 15:13 reminds us that no greater love exists but that a person will lay down one's life for friends. Paul explains to us in Romans 5:10 that while we were enemies of God, Jesus died for us. Jesus gave his life for his friends, even while they were yet enemies! Abraham was called God's friend (2 Chronicles 20:7).

---

54. Oden, *Welcomed*, 105.
55. Pohl, *Living*, 7.
56. Ibid., 26.
57. Ibid., 26.
58. Pohl, *Living*, 51.
59. Ibid.
60. Pohl, *Making*, 179.
61. Heuertz and Pohl, *Friendship*, 102.
62. Ibid., 103.
63. Ibid., 19.

Hospitality—Grace Expressed, Received, and Shared

Jesus calls his disciples friends (John 15:7–17). Jesus was a friend of sinners and tax collectors (Matthew 11:19 and Luke 7:34). Jesus calls us friends!

Friendship erodes alienation. Friendship opens people's ability to receive hospitality and things necessary to flourish. Is the decline in American churches a result of the church wanting to be known for what it is against more than it is to be like Jesus, a friend of sinners? Why would the stranger and traveler want to stop by a church where the stranger does not feel welcomed? Why would a person enter a perceived place of hostility? In reality, friends of God will love those whom God loves.[64] God loves enemies—even to the point of making them friends.[65] God goes out of God's way to befriend and to protect those who are pushed to the margins, those the religious exclude, and those the economically and politically powerful exclude.[66]

Gift Giving and Generosity are also important traits of hospitality. The biblically hospitable person will keep a light hold on material possessions and will attempt to live a simple lifestyle.[67] John Wesley viewed that anything we possess beyond what we need was not ours.[68] In fact, Wesley believed that self-indulgent, uncaring use of resources steals life from the poor.[69] Wesley further believed that taking the time to visit with the poor would provoke feelings of sympathy for the poor, which would result in taking greater action to meet the needs of the poor.[70]

Being generous with both time and resources requires an open heart.[71] Gift giving is the way we open ours and others hearts up so new relationships can be created. [72] When we give gifts, the guest becomes relaxed and open to a potential new relationship. We see God demonstrating this desire for new and restored relationship as we see how generosity describes the very disposition of God's grace.[73] Grace is a demonstration of God's lavish generosity. As we have discussed, the Trinitarian Godhead practices a

---

64. Heuertz and Pohl, *Friendship*, 30.
65. Ibid.
66. Ibid.
67. Pohl, *Making*, 12.
68. Heuertz and Pohl, *Friendship*, 56. Also see, J. Wesley, "Causes of the Inefficacy of Christianity," *The Works of John Wesley*, vol. 7, 281.
69. Ibid.
70. Ibid., 58.
71. Pohl, *Making*, 13.
72. Meeks, *Economist*, 119.
73. Carder and Warner, *Grace*, 66.

self-emptying love. A love that does not withhold. In Jesus Christ, we see the ultimate act of generosity in his life, death, and resurrection. In order to gain a biblical understanding of gift-giving and generosity, one could examine the life of Jesus for ways in which to improve these methods of expressing hospitality in their own ministry contexts.

Risk-taking is essential to biblical hospitality. Both the guest and the host take risks in hospitality. There is a risk to one's health, property, and social standing.[74] Just like God took a risk in creating a world with free will, we take risks in offering and receiving hospitality because of free will. We may be rejected, injured, judged, or taken advantage of. There is no perfect resolution to this risk or misuse of hospitality.[75] We must conclude though that to withhold hospitality is worse than the potential risks in offering hospitality.[76] Again, if we look at the risk Jesus took at being born into our world, then we must conclude from Jesus' example that the risk of hospitality must be taken.

Promise keeping makes hospitality viable and faithful. As hosts, we must understand that many of our guests are damaged, hurt, and weary from the journey of life. It is through promise keeping and being faithful that these injured, wounded guests can, over time, respond to our faithfulness.[77] People frequently experience unfaithfulness and broken promises.[78] These same people are distracted and may even abandon the porch of God when they experience the same from the church. In relational discipleship, the discipler understands that she is like God when she makes and keeps promises.[79] Promise-keeping is the integral framework of every relationship.[80] It provides the guest with hope because by faithfulness she can count on the relationship.[81] Promise-keeping is not just displayed by our verbal promises but also our faithful actions.[82] People pick up on whether they can count on us or not by our faithful or unfaithful actions.

---

74. Oden, *Welcomed*, 132.
75. Pohl, *Making*, 149.
76. Ibid., 14.
77. Pohl, *Living*, 168.
78. Pohl, *Living*, 84.
79. Ibid., 62.
80. Ibid., 63.
81. Ibid., 64.
82. Ibid., 168.

Hospitality—Grace Expressed, Received, and Shared

Truthfulness, like promise keeping, gives a foundation for the relationship. Truthfulness in relational discipleship will seek to build others up with truth instead of tear others down with it.[83] Ephesians 4:1–15 reminds us that we should speak the truth in love. Speaking the truth in love requires us not only to speak the truth, but attempt to discern the whole picture.[84] To discern the whole picture implies that we must know the truth about each other.[85] Knowing this whole picture includes understanding what all has gone into where the person before us is now. We would need to know all the experiences, education, abuses, hurts, trauma, decisions, and heredity that has brought the person to the place she is now. Most of the time, we do not know the entire truth about a person or her life situation, so it is important to have the wisdom to know when to speak and when to trust that God is at work.[86] Truthfulness does not just know the truth. It involves submitting our lives to the truth.[87] Our ultimate Truth is found in the life, death, and resurrection of Jesus Christ. Truthfulness also involves fidelity and integrity. Biblical hospitality cannot exist outside of truthfulness.

Reducing Strangeness is another key trait of hospitality. Strangeness on both the part of the host and guest causes both to feel ill at ease.[88] It is not the primary task of the guest to reduce strangeness. The host must work diligently to reduce this tension. Strangeness is reduced by attentive service to the guest making the guest feel like family.[89] We reduce strangeness when we do not make the guest feel like we are doing them a favor, but instead assure them they are conferring the favor on us.[90]

Strangeness is associated with the lens with which we view people. When we can truly see the stranger as being created by God, strangeness will begin to fall away.[91] The lens through which we see the world, our worldview, affects our judgments about the people and cultures that we encounter. We can never fully know all the situations, choices, and wounds that have affected the stranger's life. When we abandon judgments about

---

83. Pohl, *Living*, 114.
84. Ibid., 115.
85. Ibid., 122.
86. Ibid., 152.
87. Pohl, *Living*, 116.
88. Oden, *Welcomed*, 105.
89. Ibid., 105.
90. Ibid., 105.
91. Ibid., 52.

people, we can then begin to feel their loneliness, fear, pain, and emptiness.[92] Once we begin to take these different life experiences into consideration, we can begin to see these people as being fundamentally like us.[93] Finally, we reduce strangeness as we look for connections between ourselves and the guest.[94] We will certainly decrease our pattern of exclusion when we focus on the connections and the common ground we share as opposed to focusing on the strangeness of another.[95]

Safety for the Stranger and the Host is an essential component of biblical hospitality. Space we create for the stranger needs to be a safe, personal, comfortable space.[96] This place needs to offer respect, acceptance, and friendship, a place where we listen and share stories.[97] Guests are tired and wounded, and they need to have a safe place to heal and rest.[98] Some boundaries are needed to protect guests and preserve workers.[99] What is not needed is fortified walls and watchtowers ready to attack and defend against travelers. We do not need gatekeepers and locks on the doors. The boundaries need to be somewhat ambiguous and porous because we are already aware God is working in the people who approach us.[100] We will explore further how the church often defines boundaries too closely, guards the gates, and erects walls around God's grace in the next chapter.

Realizing the Outcome Belongs to God is also an important trait of hospitality. We must not measure hospitality by end results. Biblical hospitality is, instead measured by the degree to which one offers genuine presence to another.[101] Relational discipleship does not measure success in terms of how many are discipled, rather, it is measured by the depth and quality of opening our lives up for the stranger to live with us. The purpose of engaging in hospitality is not with the intention of changing the guest. Our goal in hospitality is to allow God to work as God is already working. Our

92. Boyd, *Repenting*, 15.
93. Pohl, *Making*, 98.
94. Ibid., 97.
95. Pohl, *Making*, 97.
96. Ibid., 13.
97. Ibid., 13.
98. Ibid., 140.
99. Ibid., 139.
100. Ibid., 141.
101. Oden, *Welcomed*, 109.

sole task is to walk alongside the stranger through our hospitality so the stranger may rest and be healed.

The Four Stages of Hospitality[102]

We have laid a firm foundation for understanding biblical hospitality. Without practical application, this understanding means nothing. There is a process that can be identified in the process of biblical hospitality. This process consists of four distinguishable parts. This process can be observed in God's hospitality toward us. Additionally, it matches the Wesleyan way of salvation. It also serves as a guide in our offering hospitality toward others.

The first stage of practicing hospitality is the welcome.[103] This welcome needs to be joyous and warm. The welcome does not wait for the stranger to approach, rather, it demands that the host metaphorically gets up and runs to welcome the stranger as the Father did the prodigal son (Luke 15:20). A welcome can be words of welcome or encouragement, a warm embrace, or an act of sanctuary to someone in danger.[104] A welcome never focuses on the differences nor exaggerates the strangeness of others.[105] The welcome needs to match the welcome God has extended to us.

The second stage restores the guest.[106] This restoration can include addressing either physical or spiritual needs. Again, when we look at the hospitality the Father showed the prodigal son, the Father restored the son before the son ever arrived home and before the son could complete his confession. Then, the Father proceeded to throw a lavish feast for the son. Our hospitality to others should be no less than our Father's hospitality for us. Some restoration may take time, but it should be pursued with all lavishness.[107]

The third stage involves the host and stranger dwelling together. This dwelling together is the act of sharing one's life with the other.[108] This dwelling together does not necessarily imply an actual physical living together, but it refers to doing life together where there are multiple life connec-

---

102. Oden, *Welcomed*, 145.
103. Ibid., 146.
104. Ibid., 146.
105. Pohl, *Making*, 97.
106. Oden, *Welcomed*, 146.
107. Oden, *Welcomed*, 146.
108. Ibid., 146.

tions. This is where discipleship and ministry are mundane and messy. The realities of life are shared together. Dwelling together is where real transformation begins to occur.

The final stage is the stage of sending forth.[109] This stage involves both a missional concept and a release of expectations on the stranger who has become a guest. At some point, the host must be willing to let go of the outcome. The guest may respond well to the hospitality and find healing and transformation. The guest may not respond well to the hospitality and decide to leave this place of hospitality. Yet, others may respond well and in turn become a host themselves. The outcome must be given over to God and the guest. The guest at some point may no longer be dependent on the hospitality of the host and may be able to move on. This moving on may be a release from physical help or could be sending forth for the stranger to become a host sharing hospitality.

Within these stages of biblical hospitality, a cycle perpetually exists. This cycle strengthens and deepens hospitality as this cycle is engaged. The cycle involves God's grace, our gratitude, and gift giving.[110] In fact, Paul communicates this cycle in 2 Corinthians 8–9. We breathe in God's grace, and then we exhale gratitude toward God. In this life of gratitude, we proceed to gift to others the gift of grace God has given us. As people experience God's grace through us, the cycle begins again. This is sharing the Good News of the Gospel. It can only occur in a state of gratitude and then gifting the grace that has been shared with us to others. We will find the stages of hospitality and cycle of grace helpful as we move forward in implementing and using the means of grace.

Relational Discipleship Begins When One is Awakened

Because of biblical hospitality, relational discipleship begins at the first sign of a person being awakened to God. An awakened person is a person who has an initial awareness of God and a desire for God in her life. Traditional evangelism has often emphasized belief before belonging.[111] Relational discipleship invites the awakened person "to gather and engage in service and discipleship" prior to belief.[112] This assumption is recognizing that practice

109. Oden, *Welcomed*, 147.
110. Pohl, *Living*, 24.
111. Blevins and Maddix, *Discovering*, 212.
112. Ibid.

actually often precedes belief. Therefore, hospitality embraces the notion that people can and should belong prior to belief. Hospitality invites people to come and see just as Christ's initial invitation in the gospels was to come and see.

In the parable of the prodigal son, the father did not wait for the son to get all the way home. The Father, in hospitality, ran toward the son to help the son on the journey back home. Relational discipleship compels the discipler to run toward the awakened child before the child makes it all the way home. The relational discipler meets the child while still afar off and helps the child journey back home to the house of God.

Hospitality in Relational Discipleship

We have covered a lot of ground surrounding the concept of biblical hospitality. Hospitality is essential in relational discipleship for several reasons. As we proceed further in this book, we will find that hospitality is what "bridges theology with daily life."[113] It is hospitality—both in our receiving and extending—that enables God to transform us and others.[114] Our consideration of hospitality has demonstrated that it doesn't matter what laws we keep if we do not love (1 Corinthians 13).[115] Thus, the notion is reinforced that discipleship models that do not include biblical hospitality are nothing more than religious noise.[116] Relational discipleship goes beyond this religious noise by focusing on authentic transformation through the hospitality of practices like sharing meals and stories with each other or what we call examples of means of grace.[117] Finally, relational discipleship embraces hospitality because transformation happens slowly and unevenly.[118] With the willingness to share stories and the added recognition that transformation is slow and uneven, relational discipleship garners a trust between the discipler and the person being discipled, where confession and accountability can exist.[119]

---

113. Pohl, *Making*, 8.
114. Oden, *Welcomed*, 119.
115. Boyd, *Repenting*, 56.
116. Ibid., 57.
117. Heuertz and Pohl, *Friendship*, 80.
118. Ibid., 133.
119. Boyd, *Repenting*, 220.

4

The Class Meeting—
Help for the Journey Back Home

Isaiah 35 (NIV)

The desert and the parched land will be glad;
the wilderness will rejoice and blossom.
Like the crocus, 2 it will burst into bloom;
it will rejoice greatly and shout for joy.
The glory of Lebanon will be given to it,
the splendor of Carmel and Sharon;
they will see the glory of the Lord,
the splendor of our God.
3 Strengthen the feeble hands,
steady the knees that give way;
4 say to those with fearful hearts,

> "Be strong, do not fear;
> your God will come,
> he will come with vengeance;
> with divine retribution
> he will come to save you."

5 Then will the eyes of the blind be opened
and the ears of the deaf unstopped.
6 Then will the lame leap like a deer,
and the mute tongue shout for joy.

Water will gush forth in the wilderness
and streams in the desert.
7 The burning sand will become a pool,
the thirsty ground bubbling springs.
In the haunts where jackals once lay,
grass and reeds and papyrus will grow.
8 And a highway will be there;
it will be called the Way of Holiness;
it will be for those who walk on that Way.
The unclean will not journey on it;
wicked fools will not go about on it.
9 No lion will be there,
nor any ravenous beast;
they will not be found there.
But only the redeemed will walk there,
10 and those the Lord has rescued will return.
They will enter Zion with singing;
everlasting joy will crown their heads.
Gladness and joy will overtake them,
and sorrow and sighing will flee away.

The Good King

It had been a hard battle. As the king looked out across his kingdom, his heart broke as he saw the destruction his people brought on their own land. The good king was able to survive the uprising his people raged against him and each other in their rebellion. As he continued to look across the kingdom, he could still feel hope. The people did not totally destroy his creation. He even spotted wounded people struggling to get out of the rubble. Other people were lying either dead or unconscious. Could he rescue his people and his kingdom?

The king has always wanted only the best for his people. his intent was to enable them to flourish and to enjoy his kingdom. Yet, his beloved people, at some point in time, began to question his motives. They became centered on their individual pursuits. In their questioning, the people stopped visiting the king and began to isolate themselves from him. They even began to be alienated from each other.

Relational Discipleship

He used to have a practice of regularly visiting each person and to enjoy a good walk and conversation with them. In these visits, he would find out what each person needed and would graciously send the support that person requested. He generously shared from the abundance of his kingdom. Now, people would see him coming and run into their homes and hide behind their doors. He would call out to each person by name, but the people would continue to hide. He couldn't understand why his people, whom he loved greatly, would reject him. They refused the king's support and care. Over time, the people of this kingdom became alienated from the king.

He was not the kind of king to use force. He could have easily broken their doors down and discovered how they were hiding from him. The king could have used his power to coerce the people to visit him, accept his help, and pay their respects to him. However, this king did not abuse his power in order to win the affections of the people. Instead, the king sought their love by extending hospitality to them. He knew that if he resorted to force, people would not truly love him in return. With forced subjugation, they might have given glory and praise to this king. However, they would not have truly loved the king. He hoped that over time, love would win.

In their alienation from the good king, they feared for their lives and began to take resources and life from each other. Hostility increased to the point that more violent attacks against each other ensued. Finally, there was a huge explosion. People were wounded. Some were buried under the rubble. As the king continued to look out across his kingdom, he surveyed the destruction and began to determine a plan to save his people. At that moment, his firstborn son approached the king and saw his father's heart breaking.

It was amazing how much this son resembled his father. One could not tell the difference between the two. They looked and acted like each other and even loved the same things. The people of the kingdom were loved greatly by the king and his son. The son told the father how he would be willing to go into the war-torn land to rescue the people. The father and son agreed to this plan even though the rescue attempt could cost the son's life. They loved the people so much they were willing to risk the life of the son.

There's a highway that the king maintained between the people and his home. He always kept this way clean, repaired, and beautiful. The king's intent was always to provide a safe journey to his home. He wanted his

The Class Meeting—Help for the Journey Back Home

people to have easy access to him, and he could go out to where his people were. However, this highway was damaged by the people. The fighting caused clutter, debris, and craters. Fallen trees blocked the highway in some areas. The highway was no longer easy to navigate or safe to travel. In spite of the potential danger and the condition of the highway, the son set out to make the trip.

The son endured great hardship during this journey. He made necessary repairs and cleared debris from the highway to make travel between the people and his father possible once again. Even in the midst of chaos and destruction, the son's heart was full of love for the people, and this love provided the strength he needed to complete the journey. He traveled throughout the kingdom, and he reached out to everyone he could. He offered healing and support where it would be accepted.

In the midst of death and chaos, there were still people who wanted to live free from the king. These people feared the king and chose alienation over the king's offer of healing through the son. Their resentment of the king resulted in them capturing and executing the son. The son had the resources and authority to stop this execution, but he, being like his father, expressed love continually to his father's people. He too hoped that love would win.

Before the son was executed, he connected deeply with about a dozen of the people. These dozen people were awakened by the son's love and to the king's true intent for the kingdom. These newly restored followers decided to continue the work of the son. Their mission was to help restore the father's kingdom, rebuild the king's highway, and restore access to the king's home.

The king was heartbroken to hear how his son was rejected and executed. This reality only strengthened the king's continued love and determination to restore the relationship between his people and himself. There was a sense of hope that was restored to the king when the twelve people found their way back to the king's home as a result of his son's death. He pledged and gave all the resources that were needed for the dozen to rebuild the highway and to bring the people back to the king's home.

His only requirement was that the dozen people should love his people with the same love he and his son had toward the people. A love that would extend to laying down one's life for these people. These followers were to use all the resources provided by the king, except they could never use force or power over to bring the people to a proper awareness of the king. The king wanted the people to love him, his son, and these restored followers on their own.

The king authorized these twelve to care and provide for all the needs of the people. The twelve were to make sure there was water to drink, available food and shelter, to care for the injured and sick, and to educate others so that they would share the king's story and continually reach out to his people. The twelve were to focus also on rebuilding and clearing the king's highway. As people were awakened to the king's love for them, some of the twelve were to help these awakened people travel the highway to the king's home. The twelve were to help carry belongings, advise what baggage to leave behind, give encouragement on the journey back, give direction to prevent people from getting lost, and keep people's eyes focused on the beautiful home of the king off in the distance.

Eventually, the twelve turned into three thousand restored followers of the king. Daily, more and more people, would come to their senses and realize the king had been their friend all along. The newly restored followers were committed to rebuild the kingdom, maintain the king's highway, and help people on their journey back to the king's house. Alienation between the king and his people was being overcome, and the boundaries of his kingdom expanded rapidly. The king's loving rule returned to much of the kingdom. This reality would have never happened if it had not been for the loving king and his son. However, the king was also able to depend on the restored followers who helped maintain the king's highway and helped people journey that highway back to the king's home.

> Walking in the King's Highway
> We shall see the desert as the rose, Walking in the King's highway;
> There'll be singing where salvation goes, Walking in the King's highway.
> We shall see the glory of the Lord, Walking in the King's highway;
> And behold the beauty of his Word, Walking in the King's highway.
> There the rain shall come upon the ground, Walking in the King's highway;
> And the springs of water will be found, Walking in the King's highway.
> There no rav'nous beast shall make afraid, Walking in the King's highway;
> For the purified the way was made, Walking in the King's highway.
> No unclean thing shall pass o'er here, Walking in the King's highway;
> But the ransomed ones without a fear, Walking in the King's highway.
> There's a highway there and a way, Where sorrow shall flee away;

And the light shines bright as the day, Walking in the King's highway.[1]

Here is another story that reveals some similarities with our loving Father and his desire to restore the kingdom, to keep the king's highway clear and in good repair, and to help people as they journey back to God's house. No analogy can do justice and describe fully who God is and what God is doing. However, there are some important similarities with the story of the king's highway that match a relational discipleship's focus on small accountability groups traditionally called "class meetings."

History of the Class Meeting

Before I jump into the history of the class meeting, I will provide a brief overview of what the scriptures say regarding discipleship groups. First, let us recall the way in which the Trinity functions as a small group. I examined in chapter 1 how the Trinity exemplifies a well-performing small group by interacting and serving in mission to others. Next, we see how Jesus used small groups to disciple others.[2] Throughout the gospel accounts, we find Jesus engaging with the twelve disciples, and also engaging with followers in small house groups. When reading the accounts of the early church, the central discipling group tends to be the house church.[3] Hospitality was held in high esteem in both the house church and in Jesus' small group interactions.[4] In considering the history of John Wesley's class meetings, it is important to recognize the origin of the concept in biblical and early church practices.

Wesley had this to say about the state of the Anglican Church during his time and what had developed with the Methodist's class meetings:

> Who watched over them in love? Who marked their growth in grace? Who advised and exhorted them from time to time? Who prayed with them and for them, as they had need? This, and this alone, is Christian fellowship: But alas! Where is it to be found? Look east or west, north or south; name what parish you please: Is this Christian fellowship there? Rather, are not the bulk of the parishioners a mere rope of sand? What Christian connection is

---

1. Florence Horton, "Walking in the King's Highway."
2. Raschke, *The Next Reformation*, 154.
3. Watson, *Class Leaders*, 1.
4. Oden, *Welcomed*, 216.

Relational Discipleship

there between them? What intercourse in spiritual things? What watching over each other's souls? What bearing of one another's burdens? We introduce Christian fellowship where it was utterly destroyed. And the fruits of it have been peace, joy, love, and zeal for every good word and work.[5]

These powerful words highlight the shortcomings of the discipleship practices of the Anglican Church, and they highlight the benefit of utilizing Wesley's class meeting structure for discipleship. Here is another quote of how Wesley measured the benefits of the class meeting:

It can scarce be conceived what advantages have been reaped from this little prudential regulation. Many now happily experienced that Christian fellowship of which they had not so much as an idea before. They began to "bear one another's burdens," and naturally to "care for each other." As they had daily a more intimate acquaintance with, so they had a more endeared affection for each other. And "speaking the truth in love, they grew up into Him in all things.[6]

Wesley made it clear that every Methodist was required to be part of a class meeting. He states, "Those who will not meet in class cannot stay with us."[7] Wesley drew from personal experience about the importance of the class meeting. He communicates his concern this way:

I was more convinced than ever, that the preaching like an Apostle, without joining together those that are awakened, and training them up in the ways of God, is only begetting children for the murderer. How much preaching has there been for these twenty years all over Pembrokeshire! But no regular societies, no discipline, no order or connexion; and the consequence is, that nine in ten of the once-awakened are now faster asleep than ever.[8]

He adds by saying this:

I am more and more convinced, that the devil himself desires nothing more than this, that the people of any place should be half-awakened, and then left to themselves to fall asleep again.

---

5. J. Wesley, *The Works of John Wesley*, vol. 8, 251.
6. J. Wesley, *The Works of John Wesley*, vol. 8, 254.
7. J. Wesley, *The Works of John Wesley*, vol. 13, 13.
8. J. Wesley, *The Works of John Wesley*, vol. 3, 144.

Therefore I determine, by the grace of God, not to strike one stroke in any place where I cannot follow the blow.[9]

The class meeting was an essential structure, and it provided a means of grace for Wesley and early Methodism.[10] Wesley understood that when people are left to themselves, they are inclined to fall back into destructive patterns and lifestyles. As one studies Wesley's ecclesiology, one discovers that the class meeting was one of the defining aspects of Wesley's practical theology. We could speculate and suggest that early Methodism could not have been as successful as it was without class meetings. George Whitefield, John Wesley's Calvinist contemporary, has been credited with saying this about Wesley's class meeting, "My brother Wesley acted wisely. The souls that were awakened under his ministry he joined in class, and thus preserved the fruit of his labor. This I neglected, and my people are as a rope of sand."[11]

John Wesley lived a disciplined and methodic lifestyle. This lifestyle impacted his ministry and the development of his Methodist societies. In fact, the label Methodist was first a term of ridicule by opponents of Methodism for its very methodic, disciplined ecclesiology.[12] We see, in the "disciple-making machine" that Wesley developed, a serious approach to accountability and implementation of the means of grace.[13]

The class meeting was originally not intended to be a means of discipling new believers. Wesley was concerned about how to pay down debt in the societies in 1742.[14] It was suggested that the society be divided into classes of twelve people. The class leader would go around every week to each member of the class to collect an offering for the debt. Soon, these class leaders brought reports back to Wesley about the spiritual and physical conditions of the class members.[15] Eventually, it became more prudent for the class to meet once a week rather than the class leader meeting each

---

9. J. Wesley, *The Works of John Wesley*, vol. 1, 416.

10. David Lowes Watson includes many historical documents recounting the class meeting in the Methodist Episcopal Church in the Appendix of *The Early Class Meeting: Its Origin and Significance*. The documents range from the early 1700's all the way through 1860.

11. Wood, *The Burning Heart John Wesley*, 188.

12. J. Wesley, *The Works of John Wesley*, vol. 8, 248.

13. Payne, *American Methodism*, 17.

14. J. Wesley, *The Works of John Wesley*, vol. 13, 259.

15. Ibid.

person individually. Through these developments, the class meeting became the essential and basic component of Wesley's discipleship program.

Wesley understood that the goal was not to get as many people to say the sinner's prayer as possible but to get people to follow Jesus continually.[16] He recognized the challenge of not just getting people to make a decision in a moment of conversion, but for these people to be able to live that decision out moment by moment for the rest of their lives.[17] As Wesley saw these early Methodists live, he became aware how the world could distract disciples away from God. In developing the class meeting, John Wesley desired to provide the support and nurture people needed to help them overcome the lure of the sinful world around them.[18]

The goal of the class meeting was to help people recognize God's active grace, and then to be held accountable for their responses to that grace.[19] Wesley required questions to be asked of each class member each week in order to help them consider the work of God in their lives. The questions were centered on giving an account of the previous week based on *The General Rules*.[20] The questioning was not to invite an intense confession, but rather a simple reflection of the previous week.[21] The class member could share a struggle with a particular sin without having to provide the specific nature of the sin.[22]

Wesley's desire was to keep admission into the class meeting uncomplicated. The only requirement for admission into a class meeting was "a desire to flee the wrath to come and to be saved from their sins."[23] We can see that Wesley intended discipleship to begin with people who were awakened to God. Additionally, the class members were to give an accounting of their lives by reflecting on *The General Rules*. These three rules were: "Do no harm, by avoiding evil of every kind, Do good; by being in every kind merciful after their power, and Attend upon all the ordinances of God."[24] Finally, the only other requirement Wesley had for class members

---

16. Watson, *Blueprint*, 37.
17. Ibid., 38.
18. Ibid.
19. Ibid., 43.
20. Knight, *Presence*, 100.
21. Ibid.
22. Ibid.
23. J. Wesley, *The Works of John Wesley*, vol. 8, 250.
24. Ibid., 269.

was actually to attend the class meetings.[25] Wesley understood that the accountability structure would be a means of grace for people to advance in their Christian lives, so he knew he could keep the requirements simple and clear.

People were essentially giving a testimony each week, which often resulted in other class members experiencing conversion by their participation in the class meeting.[26] This fact demonstrates why people with different experiences of God's grace should all meet together. The testimonies help others to see the way ahead on the highway back to God's house. Class members found encouragement, solidarity, advice, wisdom, and direction from the sharing of each other's testimonies.

Class meetings followed a typical pattern. The meeting would start with prayer and a hymn. Then the leader would share how the leader experienced God in the previous week and how the leader fared in following *The General Rules*. Next, the leader would begin to ask each class member about the state of their souls and how they kept the rules the previous week. During the questioning, the class leader and other members would offer encouragement, advice, and prayer for the responding class member. Each person had an opportunity to share the state of his or her soul. The class meeting would then close in prayer.[27]

Wesley's class meeting, by way of meeting in homes, recovered personal interaction and hospitality that had been lost over the course of church history.[28] As the earlier quote from Wesley indicates, Wesley recognized that key traits of hospitality were recovered through the class meeting.[29] He stated that people now experienced true Christian fellowship. These disciples were bearing one another's burdens. The intimate settings promoted mutual concern for one another. The class members did not wait for an ordained elder to provide pastoral care. These intimate connections caused people to know each other deeply. Thus, people had a greater affection for each other. Finally, Wesley recognized that in these settings, people were able to speak the truth in love to each other and by this grow in grace. The class meeting was in effect a means of helping each other journey

---

25. J. Wesley, *The Works of John Wesley*, vol. 13, 13.
26. Watson, *Class Meeting*, 26. Also see Payne, *Methodism*, 52.
27. Watson, *Covenant*, 49.
28. Pohl, *Making*, 54.
29. Watson, *Class Leaders*, 27. Also refer back to the key traits of hospitality I outlined in chapter three on hospitality.

the highway to God's house. Members helped keep the highway clear and helped others abandon unnecessary baggage. Wesley recovered a discipleship practice from the New Testament and early church, and was able to make this practice reflect the times he lived in.

The Cycle of Transformation

Wesley indicated that the main doctrines of Methodism were repentance, faith, and holiness.[30] We can correlate these doctrines to Wesley's degrees of grace: prevenient, justifying, and sanctifying grace. The graces are bestowed by God upon us, which in turn enable three responses (I will refer from here on out as degrees of faith) which Wesley indicated as being the essential or main doctrines. In the Wesleyan way, prevenient grace enables repentance, justifying grace gives people the gift of faith, and sanctifying grace leads people into holiness. I introduced earlier Wesley's analogy of the house of religion that corresponds to these graces. We can look at the house from the perspective of our response to those graces: repentance being the porch, faith being the door, and holiness being the actual rooms of the house. It all depends on whether we are considering the house from God's initiative or our response. Both are faithful ways of understanding relational discipleship and moving into God's house.

I propose a way of considering these three doctrines as being a circular, continuous action. I will suggest that holiness produces repentance. Repentance produces faith. Then faith produces holiness. The cycle continues. Further explained: God's holiness creates in us the ability to recognize we are not what we were intended to be.[31] This recognition helps us admit our condition and creates a desire to reflect the holiness we see. Holiness by its very nature creates distance because we see we are not totally "there" where God is in holiness.[32] God is distant. At the point of repentance, God's love reminds us of how close God is despite this distance. This same love seeks communion. This communion enables our faith. Our movement of faith generates a new step of holiness in our lives. Without oversimplifying the process of sanctification, I propose that this is how we are continually transformed into the image of God. We catch a new, deeper picture of God's holiness. It generates awareness where we realize we have not totally arrived

30. J. Wesley, *The Works of John Wesley*, vol. 8, 472.
31. Clapper, *Heart*, 11.
32. Collins, *Theology of John Wesley*, 21.

yet. We desire to be more like God. In love, God runs to us, embraces us and helps us along the way to internalize the glimpse of holiness we have seen. Our faith is in God helping us. God helps and empowers us, which results in our lives being changed and reflecting that holiness.

> There is a process by which people move and help others move back into the house of God. This process consists of three doctrines Wesley thought to be essential—*holiness, repentance, and faith.* [33] When we recognize holiness or perfect love in God or in others, we are brought to an awareness in ourselves where we are lacking these qualities. We are magnetized, compelled, and drawn to want to exhibit this perfect love we call holiness. This awareness helps us to admit to our lacking and creates a desire for growth to occur. This process is what repentance entails. With this awareness, confession, and desire, God enables faith in God's grace to bring about transformation. We then grow in holiness to be more like this perfect love we have experienced in God and others. Then the process begins again: holiness experienced, repentance, faith, and then holiness lived out. This process is how we move into God's house and explore the rooms of holiness in God's house.[34]

We first experience a degree of holiness that awakens us to a different way of being. This holiness or perfect love can be experienced through our interaction with God or other people who exhibit this holiness or perfect love. As a result of this awareness, we recognize the distance between our way of being and the way of holiness or perfect love that is reflected in God or another person. We experience discontent and despair when we fail to exhibit the perfect love that we seek to exude in our daily lives.

I believe the best way for people to get a glimpse of God's holiness is by experiencing the presence of God. Gregory Clapper gives two fine examples of people experiencing the holiness of God in scripture.[35] The first is Isaiah 6, where we see Isaiah experienced the holiness of God. The second example is found in Luke 5 where Peter experienced the holiness of God in Jesus. In both instances, the individuals had a profound encounter with God. Peter and Isaiah both recognized how different and distant God was from the way they were living. What is interesting is that Peter's recognition of God's holiness happened as a result of Jesus' loving action of providing fish. Jesus instructed Peter to throw the nets in a particular location. As a

33. J. Wesley, *The Works of John Wesley,* vol. 8, 472.
34. Broward and Oord, *Renovating,* 360.
35. Clapper, *Heart,* 33.

result, a massive catch of fish occurred. Peter exclaimed that he could not be around Jesus, because he recognized his own sinfulness. This action of Jesus demonstrated the loving quality, the gentleness, and the kindness of God that attracts people to God (Romans 2:4).

When we encounter God's true holiness, this other way of being can feel almost unbearable.[36] Both Isaiah and Peter were overwhelmed and expressed how this awareness was unbearable. They saw how great God was and how "undone" or sinful they were. Clapper adds, "Holiness does not increase the mess of our lives, but when we compare our lives with God's holiness we see how much bigger the mess our lives are in."[37] We are finally seeing the reality of the mess our lives really are as we compare our mess to the holiness of God. Clapper suggests that holiness allows us to see what we must do next.

Wesley viewed repentance as true self-knowledge.[38] In our place and time in society, we often view repentance as outdated and harsh. Clapper suggests that we should see repentance as Wesley did, the ability to free ourselves from self-hatred.[39] We can finally agree with God where we really are, where God already knows we are, and probably much of the world already knows as well.[40] Repentance is often being the last one to get to the party because we finally arrive at recognizing what God and others have seen all along.[41] We can finally have the courage to admit who we really are and where our lives are at in relation to God's house.

There are several dangers in how repentance is perceived or practiced. I think too often the church attempts to force a mechanical repentance. Many feel compelled to preach hell, fire, and brimstone to scare people into a decision. We preach the law to demonstrate that people have broken the law. While there is some benefit in occasionally addressing the truth of judgment and law, focusing exclusively on these truths can only produce guilt and not true repentance. People may feel condemnation rather than conviction. We cannot produce repentance, which is God's work. We are incapable of bringing ourselves to repentance. How can we think we can bring others to repentance when we cannot produce it in ourselves? Again,

---

36. Clapper, *Heart*, 43.
37. Ibid.
38. Clapper, *Heart*, 29. Also see, J. Wesley, *The Works of John Wesley*, vol. 5, 81.
39. Ibid., 32.
40. Ibid.
41. Ibid.

The Class Meeting—Help for the Journey Back Home

it is God's holiness expressed by God, or other people exhibiting this perfect love, that generates true lasting repentance.

A second danger in repentance being practiced wrongly is only going as far as having remorse.[42] Clapper notes that God wants us to repent of sin (singular). Sin is about being. Often, we think we need to repent of our sins. Yes, we should seek forgiveness for sins (wrong actions). According to Clapper, the biblical sense of repenting of sin is repenting of being out of relationship with God.[43] When we truly repent of our sin, we can also begin to eliminate our sins plural. Repentance is not saying sorry every time we commit a sin, rather, it recognizes we are not in a right relationship with God and others, and we desire to correct that fact.

From repentance, faith can well up and take action. Clapper asks us to consider the story of the prodigal son found in Luke 15.[44] As the prodigal son recognizes the distance between his current state and where the father is living, the son begins the journey home. When the father catches a glimpse of the son, the father runs to the son. The father then enables confidence or faith that the son can be whom he was once created to be and joins the son on the journey back home. The father did not wait for the son to make it home. He ran and greeted his son while his son was still a great distance from home, and then accompanied him home.

Our faith can only be enabled when we experience not just the distant, holiness, or otherness of God, but also the close, immanent, and incarnational grace of God. God sees our attempt to come back home, and God comes to where we are. God restores us and walks with us till we arrive at this new place of holiness. Clapper reminds us that faith is transitive by its very nature.[45] Faith requires an object. As we recognize God's holiness, we can then make a move toward God. Then, God's loving grace appears yet again. We can make God our object of faith and move forward in holiness. We then can have confidence in our journey because God is there beside us all along the way.

We must understand clearly that prevenient, justifying, and sanctifying graces are gifts. Repentance, faith, and holiness are in reality gifts as well. We cannot repent, have faith, and move into holiness without God's enabling. Yes, we have to cooperate and respond, but we must remember that our

---

42. Clapper, *Heart*, 38.
43. Ibid.
44. Ibid., 35.
45. Ibid., 44.

cooperation and responding are enabled and initiated by God. Any movement or recognition of God is always an act of God's prior acting grace.

A danger we encounter occurs when we think we no longer have to repent. Wesley suggested that the initial repentance that occurs at justification was a very simple and minimal repentance.[46] In reality, Wesley urged Christians to recognize their need to repent throughout their journey.[47] There is a greater degree of repentance happening after justification than there is at or prior to justification. We must believe and live in the reality that we never outgrow the need for repentance.[48] Continual repentance results in an ever-increasing depth of our faith and holiness.

What Does the Class Meeting Look Like Today?

Wesley recognized that people need help moving toward God's house.[49] I hate moving from one house to another. I think most people do because it is difficult work. People often discover they have more clutter than they should. Moving our lives spiritually into God's house by way of analogy is similar. It is more helpful to have people come along by your side to help you move. When someone is left on her own, Wesley saw that the tendency was to move back to her old life.[50] To look at it another way, when we stop responding to God's grace we will enable the "root of sin" to redevelop.[51]

One of the detrimental aspects of American Christianity has been the desire to keep religion personal and individualistic. We go to an altar and pray the sinner's prayer. We have our personal devotions. We put on our holy masks when people ask us how we are doing. We think discipleship is something completed on our own. From Wesley's perspective, this individualism was dangerous. He designed a model for discipleship that avoided this problem.

A major component of Methodism was conferencing.[52] Conferencing was intended to offer support groups at different levels that would hold individuals accountable and speak love into their lives. Wesley understood

---

46. J. Wesley, *The Works of John Wesley*, vol. 5, 81.
47. J. Wesley, *The Works of John Wesley*, vol. 5, 156.
48. Maddox, *Responsible*, 166.
49. Watson, *Class Meeting*, 50.
50. Watson, *Blueprint*, 35. Also see, J. Wesley, *The Works of John Wesley*, vol. 8, 353.
51. Knight, *Presence*, 72.
52. Clapper, *Heart*, 93.

that transformation occurs as a person recognizes and responds to God's grace. He understood that this conferencing was a means to help people do just that. Class meetings by design were Methodism's way of helping people experience and recognize grace at work in their lives. As he traveled and watched this discipling machine develop, he saw how hungry people were for God's grace. Francis Asbury had this to say about the benefits of the class meeting, "We have no doubt but meetings of Christian brethren for the exposition of scripture texts, may be attended with their advantages. But the most profitable exercise of any is a free inquiry into the state of the heart."[53]

Just as in Wesley's day, people are "hungry for grace but do not know where to find it."[54] People experience grace at "every intersection of their lives", yet, they fail to recognize the grace and the source from which it originates.[55] Unfortunately, the church has lost its ability to be recognized as the place to find grace. Relational discipleship has the ability to reclaim the church as a place to discover grace. We can do this by the re-implementation of the class meeting model that John Wesley established in which he required every member to attend.

A class meeting should not try to imitate Wesley's class meeting exactly as it was originally designed. However, its goals should correspond to Wesley's principles. The intent of class meetings is that their members experience God. The purpose of class meetings is to offer support to one another as each member experiences God.[56] The central activity of the class meeting is for members to discuss the state of their current relationship with God. The question that should be posed each week to each participant is, "How is the amazing grace of God at work in your life and relationships with other people?"[57] We should also keep in mind that the class meeting cannot save a person, but the class meeting can help people be serious and intentional about growing and to be focused on their spiritual transformation.[58]

Kevin Watson outlines some good guidelines for a re-traditioned class meeting for today in his books, *A Blueprint for Discipleship: Wesley's General Rules as a Guide for Christian Living* and *The Class Meeting: Reclaiming*

---

53. Watson, *Class Meeting*, 3.
54. Green and Greenway, *Changing*, 55.
55. Ibid., 58.
56. Watson, *Class Meeting*, 6.
57. Ibid., 12.
58. Ibid., 95.

a Forgotten and Essential Small Group Experience. I will share some of his thoughts here, but I would recommend referring to his books for a more in-depth consideration. People who desire to learn about God and want to become closer to God should be invited to participate in a weekly class meeting. The only requirements are that they are awakened to God, are willing to discuss how they see God working in their life each week and are committed to faithful attendance. The meeting should be simple, and it should not last more than an hour and a half.[59] The meeting should open and close with prayer by the class leader. After prayer, the class leader should be first to answer the question about how God has been at work. Answering first will both model how to answer and to help the other members be put at ease by the leader's openness. The class leader should then go around the group making sure each person gets a chance to answer the question. The class leader should keep the group on track by keeping answers focused and appropriate in length, so all have time to respond. If the person's answer is too long, then that person should be reminded to give others a chance to speak. The class leader can give gentle nudges to keep the answers on target and timely.[60]

While the class meeting is not a time to judge or interrogate members, the class leader should nudge a class member if the leader feels the member may not be providing specific answers.[61] The class meeting is a time to be aware and probe for greater openness. It is not a time to interrogate or judge. It is simply a time for people to recognize the active presence of God at work in the class members. It is crucial for the leader to create a safe environment if class meetings are going to be effective. The class meeting should instruct class members on various means of grace, model the means of grace, and hold people accountable for engaging the means of grace in their lives. As members answer the question about the state of their soul, the leader, and members should encourage, bear each other's burdens, advise, and pray for each other.[62]

---

59. Watson, *Class Meeting*, 105. Also see "Appendix B" in Watson, *Blueprint*, 127, for an outline of a sample class meeting. Also see my Appendix A for *The General Rules* and *Rules of the Band-Societies*.

60. Ibid., 99.

61. Ibid., 71.

62. Watson, *Class Meeting*, 85. Also see, J. Wesley, *The Works of John Wesley*, vol. 8, 254.

Essentially, people are testifying about their experiences of God each week.[63] These testimonies will often become contagious, leading other members to conversion and further experiences of God's grace.[64] The class meeting is intended to help each person cooperate with whatever grace they are experiencing, and to proceed in that grace. Class members are like brothers and sisters living in the house of religion, helping new residents enter and find their way around God's house.

This postmodern world is changing dramatically. Ideas, modes of communication, and people's values are no longer constant. People live in an unsettling time and have a deep desire for spiritual and relational components in their lives. This time is a great opportunity to offer and model relational discipleship.[65] John Wesley developed a theology centered on relational truths. God is love. God wants relationships. We are to love God and others. Grace is love in action. Relational discipleship has a powerful message to offer those living in this unsettling world. There are many theologians who see the possibility of the next great revival being centered on holiness much like the earlier Wesleyan revival.[66] God is at work in the world. Will we join God?

The church does not exist for its own members.[67] Unfortunately, it appears as if the church has forgotten that truth. God's offer of grace was costly. It cost the life of Jesus Christ. God is still a self-emptying God. In this same manner, grace is costly to the church.[68] The church must determine if it is willing to pay the price to offer that grace.

Wesley's model of the house of religion is fairly simple to understand. The goal of the Christian life is restoration of the image of God. This restoration is accomplished by repentance, faith, and holiness. Grace is the first action; love in action, God's presence inviting all people to come up to the porch of God's house. On the porch, people learn who God is. Then we hear God invite us into God's home through the door of justification. As we see ourselves as the children of God, we hear God invite us to move all of our lives into God's house as we experience sanctification.

---

63. Watson, *Class Meeting*, 26.
64. Ibid., 27.
65. Green and Greenway, *Changing*, 2.
66. Rakestraw, *Wesley*, 194.
67. Green and Greenway, *Changing*, 3.
68. Ibid., 59.

As a body of believers, we have the responsibility to help others experience the grace of God moving in their lives. We can best help the process by offering class meetings that reflect the original Wesleyan principles. The question is not whether we understand these principles, but do we have the will and discipline to put these principles into practice?[69] Are we willing to do the difficult work of keeping the King's highway free of debris, the gates unlocked and open, and help people leave baggage behind as they move toward God's house? The answer will reveal how strong our love is for God and the broken lives that live just beyond God's porch.

Fences and Baggage

There are hindrances to grace that need to be removed so people can recognize, experience, and respond to God's grace positively in each moment. In the analogy of the house of religion, we can view any fence, lock, wall, gate, or baggage as hindrances to grace that hinder access to God's porch, door, and house. These are artificial hindrances that do not match who God is and what God is doing. In our analogy of the king's highway and return to God's house, we can define these hindrances as anything that artificially blocks or impedes travel on the highway and through the gate to God's porch and door. Sometimes these barriers are created by people still outside the house of God. Unfortunately, oftentimes they are created by Christians on the other side of the fence.

In the church's concern to know who is in and who is out, the church has erected threatening fences and installed locks that turn many people away from experiencing the grace God intends for people. The church guards the perimeters making sure the unholy, wounded, and sick do not enter. People have to "say" the secret words to get past the gatekeepers of the church by affirming the right beliefs or behaviors.

David Lowes Watson indicates one major fence is erected when the church confuses salvation with discipleship.[70] When discipleship is blurred with salvation, justification becomes overloaded. Faith becomes a work. We have often misunderstood the invitation of salvation. Watson explains, "We are not inviting people to be saved, but we are informing them of their salvation and asking them to accept this reality now."[71] Justification is simply a

---

69. Watson, *Class Meeting*, 46.
70. Watson, *Foreclose*, 108.
71. Ibid., 107.

free gift already paid for by Christ. One simply needs to accept this reality. The accepting of this reality is the repentance or change of mind that God enables for justification.[72] There is no other requirement or qualification.

We lock the gates to God's house when we expect people to experience and respond to God's grace just like we did and in our timing. While we can recognize milestones in the degrees of faith and grace, we do an injustice to people by expecting them to embrace these degrees at the same time and in the same way as we have experienced in the past. Each person is unique, with each person having unique experiences, capacities, and wounds that ultimately affect how one responds to God. God's grace and the experience of God's grace are not a cookie cutter, one size fits all. Timing, capacity to recognize, abuse, addictions, other life experiences, and God's ability to know how to best initiate transformation for each person varies.

Another wall that the church erects is intellectual pride.[73] When we assume we have all the correct answers while the other person does not, places us on the same level of God. We infer that our thinking is God's way of thinking.[74] We make ourselves infallible and omniscient. We become what Wesley cautioned against: being unteachable.[75] We must not assume that it is impossible to learn from each person with whom we come in contact, regardless of their position in life or relation to God. This willingness to embrace learning from others expresses a humility that will express love and openness to relationships. This relational quality will help erode any false wall of pride.

Baggage is another type of hindrance to grace. This baggage is an artificial barrier that either has been created by the individual or by negative experiences on the journey back to God. One example of baggage is having a misconception of who God is.[76] If our mental picture of God is skewed, then how we relate to God and others will be skewed as well. In relational discipleship, friends and family in a re-traditioned class meeting can help the individual throw off the old perception of God and adopt a new view that more truly represents Christ crucified.

---

72. Maddox, *Responsible*, 162.
73. Manskar, Suchocki, and Hynson, *Understanding*, 127.
74. Ibid.
75. J. Wesley, *The Works of John Wesley*, vol. 6, 333.
76. Boyd, *Repenting*, 35.

Baggage can also take the form of physical, psychological, spiritual, and mental aptitudes.[77] Some of this baggage will require time for grace to permeate through these challenges. The baggage can be a result of hereditary, environmental, parental, economic situations, and more. Abuse, addictions, inappropriate self-image, failure, rejection, and chemical imbalances are all potential baggage. As family and friends in the re-traditioned class meeting seek to help the isolated individual, they must remember that God's grace is at work in God's time. Sensitivity to the Holy Spirit is of primary importance as group members offer mutual encouragement. We must recognize that some baggage may never be fully let go on this side of glorification.

The perimeters of the house of God needs to be unguarded with loving family of the house willing and ready to extend the hospitality to the stranger we discussed earlier. Members of the class should be on the lookout for travelers on the king's highway. The members should make sure the highway stays clear and well maintained. As soon as the members see a traveler off in the distance, the member should jump up and go out to her while she is still afar off. Restoration begins there. Help for the journey begins there. Encouragement and helping to bear the baggage of the traveler occurs at that point. In the following chapters, we will look at blockages and baggage in more depth and understand how the class meeting helps overcome and move these obstacles to God's grace through the means of grace.

Hospitality Enables the Class Meeting to Help One Move

In the previous chapter, I introduced us to the four stages of hospitality and the cycle of hospitality. In this chapter, I explained how the essential doctrines (degrees of faith) of our discipleship are really a cycle we continually experience as we move closer and further in with God. All three of these processes will help us as we understand how the class leader and members of the class meeting interact, support each other, and personally respond to God's grace.

Relational discipleship is a means of grace that occurs in a community context. It is not a model where we give someone a Bible study and then ask her to go home and complete alone. Nor, is it a class where a teacher simply provides information. Finally, it should not be optional. We should lovingly encourage all who are awakened to be part of a class meeting. The

---

77. Boyd, *Repenting*, 67.

THE CLASS MEETING—HELP FOR THE JOURNEY BACK HOME

recognition that it is not optional does not mean however that we force everyone to be part of a class meeting. We still recognize a person's free will to respond to grace. However, we should continually invite others and express the benefit of taking part in a class meeting.

Part of hospitality is recognizing where people are on the journey home to God's house. How can we run toward someone and help her on the journey if we first, do not recognize she is on the journey (awakened or unawakened), and second, where she is at on the journey? As good class members, we will learn to recognize what grace the person needs to respond.[78] Is the person receiving prevenient, justifying, or sanctifying grace? Only then will we begin to recognize how we can cooperate in God's work and we can begin to direct the person toward the next step.

The members of the class meeting can then teach, encourage, and hold people accountable for engaging the means of grace. We always keep in mind that the means of grace are not in themselves salvific. We cannot engage in the means of grace for the express purpose of earning our salvation. However, the means of grace, from a relational discipleship model, are the way we make ourselves available to God and others, and, therefore, the way we can enter into relationships with God and others.

I indicated that there were as many means of grace as there are people and moments in life. God can use whatever means God desires to convey grace to each of us. However, Wesley recognized some foundational means of grace. Wesley called these means of grace "instituted graces."[79] These included prayer, searching the scriptures, the Lord's Supper, fasting, and Christian conference. He also described another category of means of grace as "prudential graces."[80] These prudential means were things that could take different forms over time. He further differentiated between works of piety (works that point us toward God) and works of mercy (works that point us toward people).[81]

As we continue, we will see specific means of grace described and listed among God's various graces. Again, we are not providing a cookie-cutter description, rather, some practical examples of ways we can teach, encourage, and hold each other accountable will be shared. The practices of

78. Green and Greenway, *Changing*, 58.

79. J. Wesley, *The Works of John Wesley*, vol. 8, 322. Also see, J. Wesley, "The Means of Grace," *The Works of John Wesley*, vol. 5, 185.

80. J. Wesley, *The Works of John Wesley*, vol. 8, 323.

81. J. Wesley, *The Works of John Wesley*, vol. 5, 328.

the means of grace in the relational model are to experience faithfully and know the other. The means of grace in the relational model enable us to know God and other people in all ways that we can know them and in turn open ourselves up to them for them to know us as well.

Resistance to God's Grace is a Natural Process

We often get discouraged when we see people fighting or rejecting the grace God is offering. We are hopeful and want people to experience God as we have, and we can become easily frustrated or eager to give up on someone who appears to be fighting or rejecting God's grace.[82] I suggest that some resistance is a natural process of transformation. In fact, the more people are exposed to God's grace the more resistance we will witness.[83]

Until a person surrenders to God's grace, God's nudges will remain soft but persistent. These continual nudges often leave a person feeling "disturbed and unsettled."[84] I would suggest that this unsettled feeling is what in the past we often called conviction. This experience is where God's grace is working to convince us who we are, where we are, and where we need to go. Only confession will resolve this conviction. Confession is where we agree with God on who we are, where we are in life, and the direction we need to go.

As members of a class meeting, we help people on this journey of continual confession. We continually need to agree with God about ourselves in order to experience movement toward God. The class meeting exists to help create a safe place to recognize and confess our location with God.

We all experience a transitioning process when we experience God's grace calling us forward. In some degree, people will rage against God.[85] People will experience some discontent when God disrupts their lives. We do not like change, and we want to remain in our comfortable lives. As people move through the process, their next stage is grief.[86] Here, people come to terms with God's call to change. Grieving allows people to be willing to let go of old ways and embrace the future possibilities. Finally, as people move forward from grief, they are then able to embrace God's grace and

---

82. Carder and Warner, *Grace*, 36.
83. Watson, *Class Leaders*, 136.
84. Ibid., 83.
85. Watson, *Class Leaders*, 137.
86. Ibid.

in turn give God praise.[87] The more mature we are as Christians, the less stressful this transition becomes. However, it is important for members of a class meeting to recognize this process and assist people in the transition.

Conclusion

I have provided a historical account of the class meeting and provided an overall perspective of what a class meeting should look like today. In the following chapters, I will provide specific examples and suggestions regarding the four stages of hospitality, the cycle of hospitality, and the cycle of holiness, repentance, and faith (degrees of faith). These examples will not be concrete, definitive responses that should be followed as cookie cutter formats. We will discover that we should be sensitive to the Holy Spirit and to the person we are discipling. We will be reminded that it is not about how *we* experienced and responded to God's grace nor is it about what *we* think God should be doing or working on in the person's life. We must understand that God works in unique ways with each person; people respond in different ways and timing. In the very next chapter, I will help us understand that there are small steps in the journey back to God. Class meetings are simply a means of encouraging and helping people recognize God's grace in their lives, and help hold them accountable for responding to that grace.

---

87. Watson, *Class Leaders*, 137.

5

One Step at a Time

FROM THE INTRODUCTION THROUGH chapter 4, I laid the foundation for the remaining half of the book. In the Introduction, we began the discussion by presenting the predominant models of discipleship in today's American churches. Next we provided some preliminary definitions of relational discipleship. Finally, we noted why relational discipleship is important.

In chapter 1, we examined the theological characteristics of relational discipleship. We looked at how God is a relational God, who created a relational creation. Humanity made a mess of God's original home and now God, through the work of Christ, is working to bring salvation for all of creation. Taking this consideration a step further, God's work can be described as God's grace being extended to all people in every moment. This grace is always inviting each person to move one step closer toward and in God. Our responsibility is to look for God's grace and respond positively in each moment to that grace.

We previously discussed hospitality and described it as God's grace extended, received, and shared as we fellowship with one another. Hospitality is the key to the relational discipleship model. Hospitality emphasizes an approach to the means of grace as a way to know God and others. I previously suggested that one of the most effective forms of biblical hospitality are the small accountability groups known as class meetings. These class meetings become a way to extend hospitality by helping each other move back home with God. Class meetings help each other by identifying where each traveler is on the journey, helping the traveler identify and respond to God's grace through the accountable use of the means of grace, and by removing obstructions to God's grace. As we move forward from this point, we are now ready to explore practical applications of these concepts. The remaining chapters will focus on how relational discipleship takes these progressive steps.

In this chapter, we will explore in more detail the degrees of faith and grace previously discussed. We will see that there are many small steps in between crisis experiences. I will argue that we have overly focused on cookie-cutter experiences of crisis moments. We will see the importance of trying to locate the "general" locality of the traveler so that we can run toward them, help carry their baggage, and make sure obstacles are removed as they travel back home to God. Finding these locations within the degrees of grace will help us cooperate in God's work within the traveler's life instead of imposing our own agendas upon people.

Wesley's Degrees of Faith

In the previous chapters, I have described Wesley's way of salvation. On different occasions, he referred to this way as either degrees of faith or degrees of grace.[1] In the last chapter, I indicated the way in which these degrees are designated depends on the location of the action. The phrase "degrees of grace" focuses on God's action, while the designation "degrees of faith" emphasizes our reaction to these graces.

To reiterate, prevenient grace (the first degree of grace) is the grace that goes before us enabling our awakening and initial movement toward God. Prevenient grace is where our positive reaction to grace, called repentance (the first degree of faith), begins. As we continue to move forward in this repentance, God will offer justifying grace (the second degree of grace). In this offer of justifying grace, God enables our faith which brings a realization that we have been God's children all along (the second degree of faith). In this justifying grace, God will continue to draw us closer to God. The grace inviting us to live in God's presence continually is sanctifying grace (the third degree of grace). As we respond positively to this grace, we find ourselves living in God's house—living in and displaying an increasing holiness of heart and life (the third degree of faith). These movements of grace are focused on overcoming our perceived alienation from God and the effects of that alienation.

---

1. J. Wesley, *The Works of John Wesley*, vol. 12, 453. Also see, J. Wesley, *The Works of John Wesley*, vol. 10, 149.

The journey toward and in God never stops. God desires to reveal God's self to us more in each moment. God desires that we continually exhibit the holiness we experience living in God's presence. Along the journey, we will experience miraculous abundances of grace that we can describe as crisis moments as I described in chapter two on grace. These crisis moments provide profound experiences of God and considerable movement toward God. However, the majority of the journey is experienced as mundane smaller steps. While Wesley did not give specific names to these smaller steps, he did recognize that Christian transformation occurred over time.[2]

Wesley painted the broader degrees of faith in a methodic, clear fashion. He also made clear that there was an infinite variety of ways that God's grace would act in people's lives.[3] While being methodic, Wesley allowed room for God to work in any capacity God chose. As much as Wesley wanted to provide a human understanding of salvation, Wesley maintained enough fluidity in his degrees of faith to guarantee that the human effort to define theological and spiritual principles would not limit an optimistic view of God's grace.[4] He understood that if he overemphasized the degrees of faith it would create a cookie-cutter response, where people would only desire the experience and not the growth.[5] Thus, Wesley emphasized grace over degrees of faith. In his optimistic emphasis upon God's grace, he made sure that people were able to respond in their own way and in their own time to whatever measure of grace God extended to them at that moment.[6]

Unfortunately, our revivalistic heritage has created a way of salvation that emphasizes the degrees of faith over grace.[7] Especially in holiness traditions, of which I am part, our pattern of discipleship has focused upon people experiencing these crisis moments of faith (being saved and sanctified) at altars following a preaching event. I do not want to diminish these times for I have personally experienced important crisis moments

---

2. J. Wesley, *The Works of John Wesley*, vol. 5, 157. Also see the consideration of transformation over time in James K. Smith, *Desiring the Kingdom*, 226.

3. Watson, *Foreclose*, 112. Also see, J. Wesley, *The Works of John Wesley*, vol. 11, 423.

4. Watson, *Foreclose*, 112.

5. Ibid.

6. Ibid.

7. Walt, "Step 33: Let People Go Away Sad."

at altars. However, this overemphasis has created an atmosphere where a cookie-cutter process is favored over growth throughout the journey and the optimistic variety of grace that God extends.

This cookie-cutter, factory process has caused us to rely on preaching, teaching, and testimonies that support and elevate a conception of a generic one-size-fits-all operation of grace. God can and has used whatever means we make available to God. God did use this factory saving process to transform and build the church. I am concerned, however, that this process does not translate well into today's post-modern, post-denominational culture. I believe that Wesley's understanding of degrees of grace and optimism about grace, which caused him to look for and develop the accountability discipleship we see in class meetings, is the way forward for our particular time.

Wesley's optimistic view of grace was the crucial reason for his use of accountability groups. While Wesley left room for infinite experiences of God's grace, Wesley did not allow the experience and response to grace to happen by chance or in a private setting. These class meetings enabled a group to be small enough to discuss, share, encourage, and look for the infinite variety of ways God extends grace. The small group format allowed for the accountable response to that grace where people were expected to share how they responded to God's grace.[8] Additionally, people heard the testimonies of people ahead of them on the path back to God. These testimonies helped others to see the way forward toward God's house.

In many instances, it took between one to two years of membership in a class, for an awakened person to finally experience conversion.[9] This pattern is opposite of the way we have practiced evangelism and discipleship in our revivalistic heritage. Our goal has been to preach salvation and entire sanctification and expect the response of an immediate crisis experience. Wesley, on the other hand, understood that there were important smaller steps on the way to crisis experiences. He knew people needed the freedom to see and respond to God's grace as God worked in their lives.

My advisor offered a good observation as I was developing this chapter.[10] Russell Morton brought to light that Wesleyan scholars do not agree about the nature of the Aldersgate experience.[11] Was it his assur-

---

8. J. Wesley, *The Works of John Wesley*, vol. 8, 270.
9. Reuteler, *Heart*, 7. Also see, George G. Hunter III, *To Spread the Power*, p. 58.
10. Russell Morton, email message to author, June 12, 2015.
11. Outler, *John Wesley*, p. 17.

ance of salvation? Was it his sanctification experience? No one can explicitly determine where this crisis moment falls in Wesley's journey of grace. Wesley often described other people's experience of sanctification, yet we have no record of Wesley ever testifying to his own personal experience of sanctification.[12]

I think this blurring of Wesley's experience was intentional on Wesley's part. Wesley preferred to refer to salvation "as a way and not an order."[13] As an order, salvation is seen as prescribed steps in a precise order. A way emphasizes the journey while an emphasis on order emphasizes accomplishing those tasks involved in the process. When salvation is described as an order, then people tend to focus on the process and by doing so they get life from the process and not from Christ who enables the process. People, in this focus, end up having a relationship with their crisis experiences in the order of salvation. We are in danger of limiting God and excluding people when we want nice, neat, defined boundaries. In reality, salvation is a messy process of growth and transformation. As I describe practical applications of the relational disciplship model, we need to remember to be flexible and not look for an exact ordered set of responses within a particular time structure. We need to have patience and confidence in God's optimistic work of grace. We need to allow for blurred lines and varying degrees of responses based on the capabilities of people.

People in the holiness tradition typically cannot stand messy lines. We think that our holiness depends on clear boundaries—to enable them to define definitely who is holy and who is not. We need to adjust our expectations to understand that salvation is a walk with many small steps along the journey. Sometimes people step back, bounce between forward and backward steps, run ahead, slow down, stand still, get lost, or persevere forward. Only God knows all the experiences, cognitive abilities, abuse, physical and psychological limitations, education, and more, that impact a person's capability to respond to God's grace. Our goal is to understand salvation as these small steps, and to be able to locate "generally' where people are at on this journey, so that we can run toward them and cooperate with God in helping them move home with God.

---

12. Morton, email.
13. Maddox, *Responsible*, 158.

Barna Research

George Barna completed an interesting study in 2011.[14] This study took his team over six years to complete as they interviewed fifteen thousand people.[15] The focus of the study was to evaluate the spiritual transformation of people in America. The survey answers led him to define ten transformational stops people make in the course of Christian formation (see figure 1).[16]

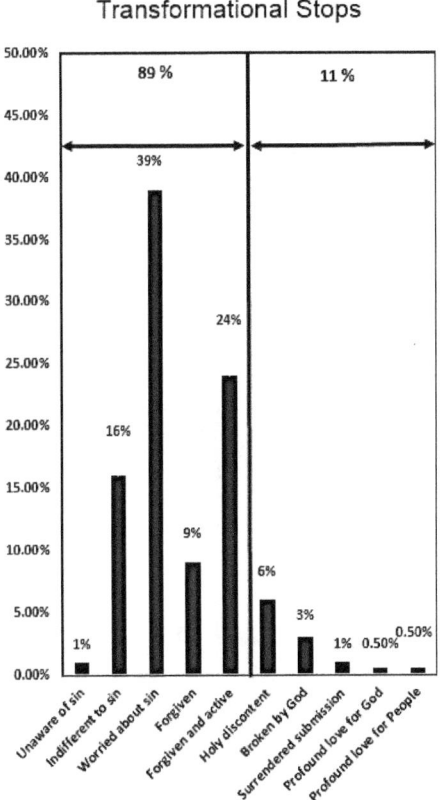

These transformational stops begin on the left with being unaware of sin and move step by step to the right until one reaches the last step of profound love for people. Barna was able to describe percentages of the respondents in each transformational step. For example, based on the survey results, Barna describes 9 percent of the people as being in an awareness of

14. Barna, *Maximum Faith*, 25.
15. Barna Group, "Research on How God Transforms Lives Reveals a 10 Stop Journey."
16. Seedbed, "About," used with permission.

being forgiven. Another example indicates that only half a percent of those surveyed experience a profound love of God.

This survey is significant in that it supports Wesley's approach to degrees of faith and grace. It adds to Wesley's insights by demonstrating that there are smaller steps in each movement toward God. If we were to break this survey into Wesley's broader degrees of grace, we find some interesting observations (see figure 2). [17]

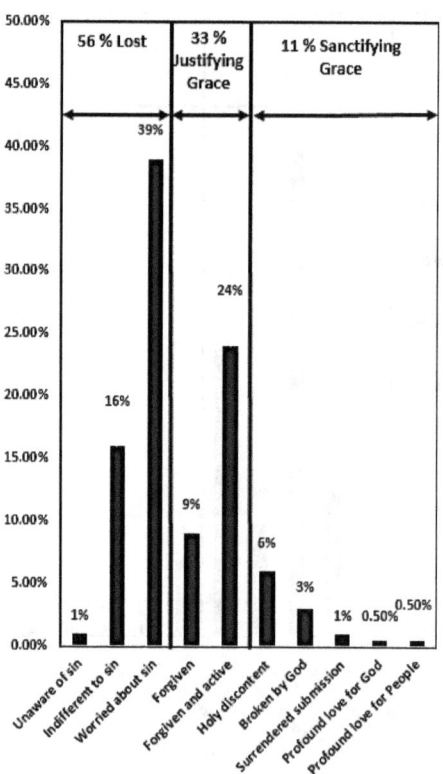

In this table, if we link Barna's stops to Wesley's degrees of grace, we see that 33 percent of those surveyed are experiencing justifying grace. This chart further reveals that only 11 percent of those surveyed move forward into sanctifying grace. While this illustration shows 56 percent as being lost, if we move back to figure 1, then we conclude that 39 percent of those lost are in some awakened state as they express they are worried about sin.

17. Seedbed, "About," used with permission.

One Step at a Time

Barna's study is helpful in many ways. First, it significantly supports a view that there are smaller steps in the move back to God's house. This study also describes some of the particular traits of these smaller steps. Some are simply states of awareness while others are definite experiences of God, and others are responses to God and others. Furthermore, we can see that God is active in all people in an infinite variety of ways. Even more, we can recognize that the harvest is ripe as only 17 percent of the population is indifferent to or unaware of sin. Finally, we can see the potential of beginning relational discipleship with awakening people. Are we willing to go where the person is at on the journey and cooperate with God to help these persons move home to God?

Engel Scale and the Gray Matrix

In my research on the nature of salvation as a process, I encountered approaches that support Barna's research on transformational stops. The first such tool is the Engel Scale. The Engel Scale was developed by James F. Engel and Viggo Søgaard and was first published in 1975 in *What's Gone Wrong With the Harvest*.[18] This scale describes the progression of the salvation process from an awareness of a supreme being all the way through repentance and into growth in Christ. This scale measures thirteen steps (see figure 3).[19]

	^	Externally (witness, social, action, etc.)
	^	Internally (gifts, etc.)
	^	Reproduction
	5	Stewardship
	4	Communion with God
	3	Conceptual and Behavioral Growth
	2	Incorporation into Body
	1	Post-Decision Evaluation
		NEW CREATURE
	-1	Repentance and Faith in Christ
	-2	Decision to Act
	-3	Personal Problem Recognition
	-4	Positive Attitude Toward Gospel
	-5	Grasp of Implications of Gospel
	-6	Awareness of Fundamentals of Gospel
	-7	Initial Awareness of Gospel
	-8	Awareness of Supreme Being but no Effective Knowledge of Gospel

---

18. Engel and Norton, *What's Gone Wrong With the Harvest?*, 45.
19. Engel and Norton, *What's Gone Wrong With the Harvest?*, 45.

Another position described the process in a two-dimensional perspective. This particular approach is called the Gray Matrix.[20] Frank Gray used an approach similar to Engel's, but with a different perspective on the progression of faith. His contribution is to provide an additional perspective, which takes into account one's openness to the Gospel. He proposes four different quadrants where people can be identified in relation to their openness and knowledge in faith (see figure 4).[21]

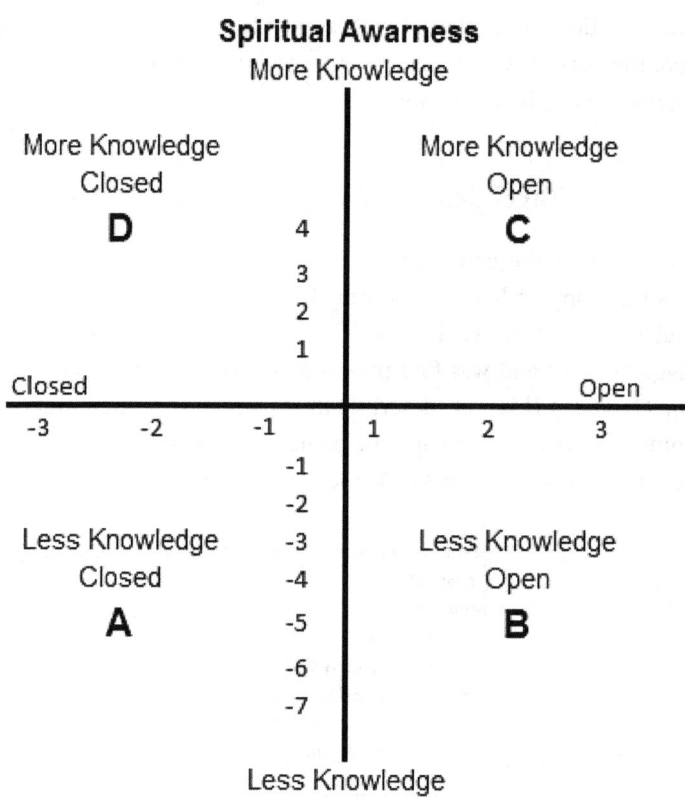

Gray's Matrix emphasizes that people's faith journey begins with little awareness of God. People in this place on the journey would be in the bottom left quadrant. As God's grace is continually active and as the body of Christ cooperates with God, people will progress both in openness and in awareness or knowledge of God. People will progress in their own unique

20. Gray, "The Gray Matrix," used with permission.
21. Gray, "The Gray Matrix," used with permission.

way into the lower right quadrant. For instance, a person may have progressed to (1,-6) where they are more open than closed to the claims of Christ. As God's grace continues to draw people to God, and people become more open to the claims of the Gospel, they will eventually cross a threshold where justification takes place. We could identify that place somewhere around (2, 1). I would suggest from a Wesleyan perspective that sanctifying grace is experienced somewhere around (2, 4). Again, we do not want to limit God's variety and operation of grace, but we want to locate "generally" people on the journey (see figure 5).[22]

The Complete Matrix Extended

More Knowledge

	6	Continuing Growth
	5	Aware of Responsibilities
	4	Knowledge of God's Kingdom
	3	Knowledge of Adoption
	2	Experience of God's Love
	1	Initial Knowledge of Father God

Closed — Open

-3	-2	-1	1	2	3

	-1	Aware of Cost
	-2	Grasps Implications
	-3	Aware of Personal Need
	-4	Aware of Basics of Gospel
	-5	Interested in Jesus
	-6	Aware of Jesus
	-7	Wonders if God Can Be Known
	-8	Vague Awareness & Belief in God
	-9	God Framework
	-10	No God Framework

Less Knowledge

We can chart one's progression in the Gray Matrix and identify it as a journey. It will be uneven and fluid depending on an individual's openness

---

22. Gray, "The Gray Matrix," used with permission.

to God's grace at any specific time. A journey could look optimistically like what is depicted in figure 6. [23]

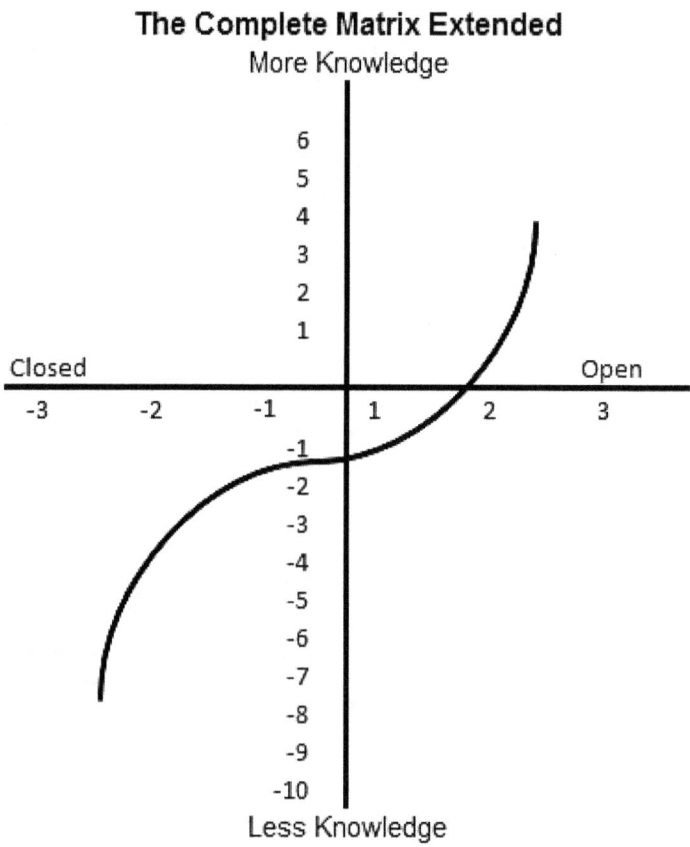

I prefer the Gray Matrix over the Engel Scale because it includes added details concerning one's openness to the Gospel. Unfortunately, as the Gray Matrix demonstrates, people who have journeyed into justifying and sanctifying grace can become closed to grace. We would find these people in the upper left quadrant (figure 4). I propose that people cannot remain in that quadrant for any length of time without also experiencing a gradual decline in their knowledge and awareness. Thus, reinforcing Wesley's view that, if a person is left on their own they often end up back in old and poor lifestyles.

23. Gray, "The Gray Matrix," used with permission.

One Step at a Time

Comparison of the Data

We will now compare the data of the Barna research and the paradigms of the Engel Scale and Gray Matrix with our understanding of the Wesleyan way of salvation. In figure 7 below, corresponding features of each paradigm are laid side by side. I have arranged the chart to demonstrate how the stages of spiritual development of each model correspond to each other. I realize there will be some disagreement about some of the precise details. However, keep in mind that my argument is not dependent upon precise order of the stages as it is the manner in which these paradigms reflect a common reality. In practice, individuals will experience these stages in different sequences. For example, two different people may experience being awakened in different stages. One person may become aware of a personal need, then become aware of the Gospel; while another person becomes aware of the Gospel before experiencing an awareness of a personal need (see figure 7).

I do believe the broader degrees of grace do occur in order, but those lines can be blurred to some extent. For example, do we have to force everyone into saying the sinner's prayer for justification to take place? Do all people have to be able to name a definitive time where they realized they were a child of God? Can all people identify one crisis moment where they began living in sanctifying grace? Again, we are more concerned about God's grace than we are trying to define and control a certain boundary or line of that experience. In the following chapters, I will provide some ways of generally locating where people are at in these graces.

Engel Scale		Seedbed/ Barna		Gray Matrix		% of Pop.
#		Pop. %		#		
	Externally - witness, social, action, etc					
	Internally- gifts, etc					
5	Reproduction Stewardship	0.5%	Profound Love for People			
4	Communion with God	0.5%	Profound Love for God			11.00%
		1%	Surrendered Submission	6	Continuing Growth	
		3%	Broken by God	5	Aware of Responsibilities	
3	Conceptual and Behavioral Growth	6%	Holy Discontent	4	Knowledge of God's Kingdom	
Sanctification						
2	Incorporation into Body			3	Knowledge of Adoption	
1	Post Decision Evaluation	24%	Forgiven & Active	2	Experience of God's Love	33%
-1	Repentance and Faith in Christ	9%	Forgiven	1	Initial Knowledge of Father God	
Justification						
-2	Decision to Act					
-3	Personal Problem Recognition			-1	Aware of Cost	
-4	Positive Attitude Toward Gospel					
-5	Grasp Implications of Gospel			-2	Grasp Implications	Awakened 39%
				-3	Aware of Personal Need	
-6	Awareness of Fundamentals of Gospel			-4	Aware of Basic Gospel	
				-5	Interested in Jesus	
-7	Initial Awareness of Gospel	39%	Worried About Sin	-6	Aware of Jesus	
		16%	Indifferent to Sin	-7	Wonders if God Can Be Known	
-8	Awareness of Supreme Being No Effective Gospel			-8	Vague Awareness and Belief in God	Unawakened 17%
		1%	Unaware of Sin	-9	God Framework	
				-10	No God Framework	

Wesleyan Way		Revivalism	Wesleyan Way	House of Religion	Triune God
God's Action - Degrees of Grace	Our Reaction - Degrees of Faith				↑ King's Highway
↑ ↑ ↑ ↑ ↑ ↑ ↑ ↑ ↑ Sanctifying Grace	↑ ↑ ↑ ↑ ↑ ↑ ↑ ↑ ↑ ↑ ↑ ↑ ↑ ↑ ↑ ↑ ↑ Holiness	Then Belong	Then Believe	House	
↑ ↑ ↑ ↑	↑ ↑ ↑ ↑	↑ ↑ ↑ ↑		Door	
Justifying Grace ↑ ↑ ↑ ↑ ↑ ↑ ↑ ↑ Convincing Grace ↑ ↑ ↑ ↑ ↑ ↑ ↑ Prevenient Grace	↑ Faith ↑ ↑ ↑ ↑ ↑ ↑ ↑ ↑ Repentance	Believe First	Belong First	Porch Woods, Shacks, Hiding	↓ Our Furthest Point of Alienation

People in a postmodern context are inclined to view salvation as more of a process and less of a crisis experience of saying a right prayer and holding the right beliefs.[24] This fact has long been understood by the broad stream of the Christian church but was lost in the revivalistic heritage of holiness churches. People understand that several encounters or touches are what nudges people forward step by step.[25] For example, Boren suggests that it takes twelve to twenty nudges to move a disciple forward in the Engel Scale.[26] Most people come to the knowledge of God in a series of encounters that nudge people forward spiritually, rather than single crisis experiences.

We are also finding that the days of individual door to door evangelism are gone. Evangelism now needs to be a community effort.[27] Postmodern people also, generally speaking, do not respond to sermon invitations exhorting hearers into crisis experiences. Greater spiritual growth and understanding occur when people are confronted in social situations. This changing environment begs us to approach discipleship relationally; that celebrates the smaller steps people make toward God's house. We cannot settle for nostalgia for the "good old days" of how we used to evangelize and disciple. Good missionaries contextualize their ministry for the culture they are trying to reach. Should we expect this new culture to accept our foreign ways? Are we ready to cooperate with God's optimistic grace and patiently walk alongside people as they travel toward God?

Crisis or Nudge?

We keep coming back to the tension between process and crisis. Is it all small steps of growth in grace? Should we focus on crisis experiences of justifying or sanctifying grace? I suggest that we intentionally allow for both experiences of God's grace. To reiterate, I have defined a crisis experience as anytime we perceive or experience a miraculous abundance of God's grace that causes us to move toward God in a demonstrable way. I do not think we have to limit crisis experiences only to justifying and sanctifying grace. We will have many crisis experiences over our journey toward God. Again, most of our journey will be the smaller, every day, persistent steps toward God.

24. O'Connell, *Compassion*, 58.
25. Carson, *Conversant*, 275.
26. Boren, *Relational*, 140.
27. Carson, *Conversant*, 275.

One Step at a Time

The problem arises when we impose on others a need to undergo a crisis experience. A person may not perceive or experience grace in the same manner we did. We need to be careful how we impose our types of crisis experiences upon others. Our revivalistic heritage has influenced how we perceive experiences. We have inadvertently made religious experience the mark of discipleship.[28] In my particular holiness heritage, we have encouraged people to testify about experiences. We want to hear people say they are saved and sanctified. This testimony provides what we want to see in discipleship. All other marks of growth and movement toward God become less important and even unnecessary. We assume the two experiences will cause the growth and will result in all of the transformation we want. We have mistakenly communicated that our initial and crisis experiences of God are central to our transformation.[29] In reality, it is the subsequent effects and steps that impact and make the most difference in our living in God.

While our crisis moments will propel us along the way, we must continually remember that transformation usually occurs unevenly and slowly.[30] Transformation is helped greatly through community and multiple continued nudges.[31] God works in the context of community to provide the gradual steps through nudges by fellow travelers extended through hospitality. People experience and respond to God's grace differently. Because we all have different experiences, what one person perceives as a crisis experience may be different from how God dealt with another. Thus, we should focus on the fruit each individual is producing. Because no one experiences God's grace in the same way, we are in no position to judge the validity of these experiences. Instead, we need to evaluate the fruit that each person's response produces along his or her faith journey. With this adjusted focus, we will be able to locate better where one is on the journey, and be in a better position to cooperate with God in nudging the person toward God's house.

---

28. Watson, *Foreclose*, 30.
29. Manskar, Suchocki, and Hynson, *Understanding*, 122.
30. Heuertz and Pohl, *Friendship*, 133.
31. Hunter, *Radical*, 35.

Relational Discipleship

The Cookie Cutter and Timer that We Bring from the Old House

As our understanding of God's grace becomes more flexible, we will need to discard our cookie cutters and timers. Again, when we focus on cookie-cutter experiences, we are asking people to conform their lives to our experiences, and not to be conformed to the Christ, who is the author of our experiences. Our model for transformation should not be cookie cutters we have handed down from generation to generation. Our model must be always and only Christ.[32] Our faith is not centered on experience, but on Christ. When we impose a cookie cutter experience, people focus on copying the experience. Instead, let us lift up Christ as the One to whom we seek to become conformed.

We further hinder discipleship with this cookie cutter mentality by focusing all our efforts on people's experiences. In reality, the experience becomes more important than the people whom we are trying to funnel through these experiences.[33] As we exalt the experiences, we the disciplers, are no longer placing our confidence in God's grace. In our misplaced confidence, our time expectations drive us. We want people to change, transform, and share experiences in our timing. It never crosses our mind that God has been and will continue faithfully to be at work leading the person toward God in ways that do not match our expectations. We want the person to jump ahead and experience the next crisis moment. Instead, we need to be faithfully and patiently walking alongside the person as she makes the smaller steps, grasping God's grace as she is capable.

As we discard our cookie cutter and our time expectations, we will perceive God's grace as it really is—vast, universal, always at work, and abundant. Again, I am not suggesting we lower expectations and not seek transformation. What I am saying is that as we faithfully conduct class meetings, the people in these groups will intentionally look for new experiences of God's grace and hold each other accountable for their responses to that grace. The class meeting provides the relational framework that enables this more optimistic view of God's grace to operate. We can tear down our false fences and unlock the gates so that God's grace can flow freely, and be experienced and responded to in unique ways. In the past, rigid cookie-cutter approaches to the work of salvation compelled us to safeguard our boundaries and place

---

32. Watson, *Foreclose*, 112.
33. Watson, *Foreclose*, 106.

limits upon God's grace. With the faithful use of class meetings, we can once again find the church as a place for grace to flow in abundance.

Barriers and Baggage

In the previous chapter, I introduced examples of some barriers and baggage that interfere with people recognizing and responding to God's grace. There are three different types of obstacles—*barriers* the church erects, *blockages* the world disrupts the journey with, and *baggage* the traveler carries throughout life. First, barriers are fences, walls, locks, gates, and improper "watchmen on the wall" (Ezekiel 3:17-19) that are established in order to protect the church's integrity, but in practice hinder the operation of God's grace. Second, blockages are institutions, mindsets, lies, temptations, and various other opposing forces to the kingdom of God that the world attempts to disrupt, damage, and otherwise block the King's Highway and the free bidirectional travel between God and God's children. Finally, individual people carry baggage that limits a person's ability to respond to God's grace. This baggage includes a wide variety of issues, like heredity, abuse, addictions, traumatic experiences, economic status, education, mental aptitudes, chemical imbalances, upbringing, and sins. We should note that just as there is an infinite variety of ways that God's grace acts there is a similar variety of barriers and baggage. While the discipler cannot control people's experience and response to grace, the relational discipler will come alongside the disciple. The relational discipler will work to keep the gates open, the fences torn down, and the highway clear of the world's debris. The relational discipler will also carry baggage by bearing the potential disciple's burdens (Galatians 6:2) and advising new believers how to abandon old life that encumbers discipleship (Hebrews 12:1).

I defined some obstacles in the previous chapter. I would also like to share a longer list of obstacles so that we can better understand how the three different categories of encumbrances block the view of God's house and limits the traveler's ability to recognize and respond to God's grace. This list will not be exhaustive. I am confident as you read the list; potential other hindrances will come to mind. Additionally, there could be some disagreement about whether a particular obstacle is really bad. Not all obstacles have to have an assigned moral value of being good or bad. I am simply naming concepts and issues that can distract or impede the free flow of God's grace. Please use this list as a springboard for envisioning even more hindrances that disciples experience in responding to God's grace.

Artificial Barriers the Church Erects

- Making the church into a military complex—a fortress mentality—more concerned about being in a defensive posture
- Judging
- Withholding hospitality
- Being watchmen on the wall for defense as opposed to watching for travelers on the journey to run toward and extend hospitality.
- Wrong or poor views of God, atonement, discipleship
- Overly focused on absolute truth
- Overly protecting non-essential beliefs
- Promoting political agendas
- Self-interest
- Practical atheism
- Legalism
- Church clichés or jargon
- Focus on self-maintenance
- Consumerism
- Civil religion
- Fearful of change
- Fearful of postmodernism
- Anti-science
- Unwilling to allow difficult questions
- Afraid holiness is fragile
- Cookie Cutter experiences
- Wanting people to change in the church's time
- Being overly known for what the church is against as opposed to a place where grace can be experienced.

- Inhospitable attitudes
- Unwilling to accept the stranger
- Making the stranger feel like the stranger has to change before they can be welcomed.
- Extending hospitality with the goal of changing the stranger
- More focused on the symptoms—sins—then on the disease—sin
- Giving false prominence to certain sins
- Giving the appearance that one sin is the deal breaker sin while not addressing the favorite personal sins of the congregation.
- Lack of humility-not taking the view of Paul—"I am the chief sinner" (1 Timothy 1:15)
- Lack of biblical hospitality
- Self-righteousness

Blockages by the World
(Alternate Roads, Attempts to Destroy or Block the King's Highway)

- Individualism
- Consumerism
- Nationalism
- Modernity
- Postmodernity
- Empire
- Pluralism
- Tolerance
- Inhospitality
- Social classification
- Economic classification
- Abuse
- Hedonism

- Competition
- Lies about God, self, and others
- Secularism
- Power over—using force over marginalized groups
- Violence
- Materialism
- Patriarchy
- Inappropriate sexualization
- Partisanship
- Temptations
- Ignoring the marginalized
- Rage
- Division
- Inequality
- Racism
- Greed

Personal Baggage (Anything the Disciple Carries Along the Journey)

- Idols
- Lies about God
- Lies about others
- Lies about self
- Judging
- Fear of being judged
- Grudges
- Broken relationships
- Pride
- Envy

- Hatred
- Addictions
- Sins
- Alienation
- Abuse
- Masks—hiding who we truly are-hypocrisy
- Hurts
- Resentment
- Anger
- Unforgiving spirit
- Traumatic experiences
- Inherited problems—social and physical—genetic and environment
- Mental aptitudes
- Education
- Economic status or stigma
- Family
- Failed relationships
- Health issues
- Doubt
- Fear
- Jealousy
- Competitive spirit
- Elevated ego
- Unfaithfulness
- Rejection
- Low self-esteem
- Failure
- Loss
- Grief

- Attitudes
- Weaknesses
- Greed
- Perfectionism

The Class Meeting and the Relational Discipler

For the remainder of this chapter, I will describe some characteristics and functions of the class meeting and the relational discipler. Relational discipleship hinges on biblical hospitality. True hospitality seeks out travelers on God's highway. This hospitality urges us to run toward the traveler and extend the key traits of hospitality I have described in chapter 3 on hospitality. This same hospitality motivates us to tear down and destroy artificial barriers the church has erected around God's house. In hospitality, we run out into the King's highway to keep it free from worldly debris. We try and make sure the signage is clear and does not point to other roads.

As we run out to the traveler, we see how burdened the traveler is as she tries to carry all the baggage she has accumulated throughout life. Some baggage needs to be abandoned. Other baggage the traveler is not yet ready to abandon. We are hospitable when we help carry those burdens until by God's grace; the traveler can finally release that baggage. In this model, priority is not placed on an experience, change, or conformity to our values. The priority is placed on the stranger, to whom God has already ascribed unsurpassable worth. Our task is to help the traveler on the journey.

The class meeting and the relational discipler act first as the highway maintenance crew. We are to keep the path straight and clear. We are to make sure the highway is safe to travel. The stranger is wounded and tired, so the stranger needs to be able to travel without fear of being attacked. The class meetings will provide a safe environment for people to develop healthy coping strategies as they face obstacles on their journey toward a covenant relationship with God. The maintenance crew will be on the lookout for obstacles that could distract people on their faith journey. The relational discipler will engage means of grace that will assist highway maintenance. Holy conferencing, prayer, searching scriptures, and fasting are among the means of grace that will maintain the King's highway.

The class meeting and the relational discipler are proper watchmen. Many people in the church today think the church needs "watchmen on the wall" to defend against attacks on the church or God. The church is not a fortress engaging in brutal battle against other people. Instead, proper watchmen watch out for travelers, as did both the prodigal's father and Abraham, as we noted in chapter 3. The class meeting and relational discipler are always on the lookout for a new traveler who has just recently become awakened to God and has started the journey home. Utilizing the means of grace help produce a proper sense of biblical hospitality. Works of mercy will focus on these watchmen going out to people with aid such as but not limited to: feeding the hungry, visiting the sick and imprisoned, clothing the naked, and giving a cold glass of water.

The class meeting and the relational discipler will engage and model active listening and confession. The only hope a wounded and tired traveler has for returning home to God will be in a safe environment where the traveler comes to an awareness that she is truly being heard. The expanded exploration of each stage will communicate practical ways the class meeting can provide this safe environment. As the traveler witnesses authentic confession among other class meeting members, she will develop the trust to be able to confess where she has come from, and what baggage she is carrying. Means of grace include good, holy conferencing that authentically practices active listening and heartfelt confession. We can see how important hospitality is as people will flourish and feel free to share their burdens in the context of the safe environment of a class meeting. (Please see the "One Anothers" found in scripture for creating a safe environment in the class meeting located at the end of this chapter).

The class meeting and the relational discipler will help the traveler move back home with God through the accountable practice of the means of grace. The class meeting engages in both modeling and teaching the means of grace to the traveler. The traveler should develop an ability to give an accountable report of the practice of the means of grace each week (referred to in the remainder of the book as the "accountable practice of the means of grace"). The traveler, through hospitality, should be made comfortable enough to report not only successes but also the failures in practicing the means of grace. The means of grace are the tools that help carry and let go of baggage in the traveler's life.

We have identified both steps and obstacles in the journey back to God's house. In relational discipleship, the goal of the class meeting is to help identify where the disciple is at on her journey, and then to run toward the disciple and walk alongside of her while removing the obstacles to

Relational Discipleship

God's grace. The relational discipler should develop an intentional awareness of the general locality of where the disciple is on the journey, and the obstacles that are hindering spiritual progress. This awareness can only occur as we maintain an optimistic view of God's grace and engage in biblical hospitality.

In this resource, I am mostly concerned with why we should do relational discipleship and the overarching themes that drive relational discipleship. There are many good resources that provide specific help in starting, organizing, and structuring the class meeting, covenant group, or sometimes called an accountability group. I would refer you to my bibliography to find the many resources that are available. Additionally, in the bibliography, you will find some good resources that further explore the historical nature of the class meeting in the early Methodist church. These resources will provide greater detail as you develop a working class meeting as you further engage in relational discipleship.

In the following chapters, the relational discipleship model will be developed more specifically as we take a chapter for each of the broader degrees of faith in the journey back to God's house: 1) the woods; 2) the porch; 3) the door; 4) the house of God. I will discuss what each of the broader degrees of faith generally look like, the smaller steps that are potentially in each broader movement, what means of grace may best serve each stage, the cycles of hospitality, grace, and faith, potential obstacles in each stage, and what some natural cycles of resistance to grace may look like. We will need to remember that the journey is slow and uneven.

The "One Anothers" Found in Scripture as Guidelines for Creating a Safe Environment in the Class Meeting

- John 13:14—Ought to *wash* one another's feet (have the mindset of serving).
- Romans 12:10—Be *devoted* to one another
- Romans 12:10—Give *preference* to one another in honor
- Romans 12:16—Be of the *same mind* toward one another
- Romans 15:7—*Accept* one another
- 1 Corinthians 12:25—*Care* for one another
- Galatians 6:2—*Bear* one another's *burdens*

One Step at a Time

- Ephesians 4:2—*Forbear* one another
- Ephesians 4:32—*Forgive* one another
- Ephesians 4:32—*Be kind* to one another
- Ephesians 5:21—*Be subject* to one another
- 1 Thessalonians 5:11—*Encourage* one another
- 1 Thessalonians 5:11—*Build up* one another
- Hebrews 10:24—*Motivate* one another to love
- James 5:16—*Confess* your sins to one another
- James 5:16—*Pray* for one another
- 1 Peter 4:9—*Be hospitable* to one another

6

The Woods

Out in the highways and byways of life, many are weary and sad.
Carry the sunshine where darkness is rife, making the sorrowing glad.

Make me a blessing; Make me a blessing. Out of my life may Jesus shine; Make me a blessing, O savior, I pray, make me a blessing to someone today.

Tell the sweet story of Christ and his love; Tell of his pow'r to forgive. Others will trust Him if only you prove true ev'ry moment you live.

Give as 'twas given to you in your need; Love as the Master loved you; Be to the helpless a helper indeed; Unto your mission be true.[1]

In chapter 4, discussing the class meeting, I began with an allegory of a king, his kingdom, and the king's highway. In this analogy, we saw how the people of the kingdom isolated themselves from the king and eventually brought great destruction to the kingdom and the king's highway. We also saw how the king's son gave his life to go into the wrecked kingdom and attempt to clear the king's highway while also helping to restore the kingdom. The action of the king's son was successful in compelling people to return to the king and to join in the restoration of the kingdom and maintaining the king's highway. The king's people also helped other people return to the king via the king's highway. They aided travelers by helping to carry baggage, advising as to what baggage needed to be abandoned, and pointing

---

1. Ira B. Wilson, "Make Me a Blessing."

The Woods

travelers in the right direction. The king's people also restored, encouraged, and provided sanctuary, and otherwise helped travelers journey back to the king's house. From this analogy, I drew a comparison as to how the class meeting is much like the help these restored citizens provided to people traveling back to the king's house.

In the remaining chapters, I will focus upon each segment of the journey back to God's house, and look in greater detail as to what is involved in those segments. As we move forward, I want to remind us that we should not look for concrete steps, defined lines, or things to happen in our time frame. Our confidence is not in the work we do, the process, or even in the response of the person who is being discipled. Our confidence must always be located in the optimistic, always at work grace of God. In this confidence, we can remain faithful to the person, regardless of the progress, or lack thereof, we perceive. We must be open to blurred lines, slow and uneven transformation, as well as miraculous moments of abundant grace that compels significant transformation along the journey.

The first location on the journey back to God's house is in what I describe as "the woods," where we hide and are lost, and "the shacks" that we create and inhabit. This location includes people who are unawakened and awakened. By unawakened, I mean people who have little to no awareness of God and little to no awareness of sin. These people can also include those who do have an awareness of God and sin but are indifferent to this awareness. This awareness level and indifference can be seen by how these people live their lives without regard to God and the implications of sin.

As God's grace begins to invite a response in the unawakened person, they begin to awaken from their slumber.[2] Just like most of us waking up in the morning, there are varying degrees of being awakened and coming to full functioning consciousness. In the spiritual realm, people often experience a similar sort of awakening experience, where they progress from experiencing little to no awareness of God and sin into a greater awareness and concern for God and sin. As we look further at this particular segment of the journey, I will also identify potential barriers, blockages, and baggage that limit or interfere with the ability to perceive and respond to God's grace positively. I will also suggest potential means of grace that can be used to help overcome and be aware of these hindrances to grace, as reflected in figure 8.

---

2. J. Wesley, *The Works of John Wesley*, vol. 5, 19.

Map of the Woods		The King's Highway	God's Action	Location	Steps to the House of God
	Works of Mercy - Feeding, Clothing, Visiting	Prevenient Grace — Awakened and Begins the Journey			Can See the House of God off in the Distance
	Masks				Understanding the Language of the Gospel
	Searching Scriptures				Aware of Jesus
	Church - Anti-Science				Wonders if God Cares About Self
	Church - Practical Atheism				Attempts to Reconcile Current State with the Gospel
	Worship				Limited Awareness of Gospel
	Church - Self-righteous				Growing Belief in God
	Church - Unwilling to Allow Difficult Questions				Longs to Return Home
	Prayer				Worried About Sin
	Class Meeting				Aware of Being Incapable of Fixing and Satisfying Need on Own
	Civil Religion			Unawakened - Lost in Woods, Hiding, Living in Shacks We Create	Attempting to Satisfy Needs on Own
	Church - Judging, Witholding Hospitality				Recognize Sin and Need in Life
	Consumerism				Limited Awareness of God
	Sins				Aware of Sin but Indifferent
	Lies About God				Aware of God but Indifferent
	Idols				No Awareness of Sin
	Secularism				No Awareness of God
	Potential Blockages, Barriers, and Baggage and the Means of Grace to Move Barriers				Steps to the House of God

(shaded)	= Barriers, Blockages, and Baggage
(unshaded)	= Means of Grace

The Woods

I refer to this depiction as the "Map of the Woods" in the journey back to God's house. The woods, where there is little to no awareness of God, is the furthest perceived and experienced alienation from God. This tool should be used as a guide for the relational discipler to "generally" locate the traveler so that the discipler can run toward the traveler in hospitality. It is essential that relational disciplers realize that this tool cannot be treated as a checklist or precise process that each disciple must follow on their journey into a deeper relationship with God. This tool provides a general framework for disciplers to guide their traveler forward on the faith journey. The discipler's job is to come alongside the traveler on the journey back to God's house. The discipler must discern where the Holy Spirit is leading them on the journey to prevent the traveler from going too far ahead, getting too far behind, or getting lost on the journey.

In the column labeled, "Steps to the House of God," I suggest various steps along the highway back to God's house. The steps may not happen in a definitive order. For instance, we may perceive that some of the steps happen all at once. On the other hand, because of one's upbringing in church, she may not have ever had a time of not being aware of God or her sin. Likewise, the sequence of potential disciples may not occur in the precise order I have outlined. The arrangement of the steps are a guide and not a definitive checklist of a predetermined process. The fluidity of the map demonstrates that each disciple has a unique journey that God is willing to interact within each moment.

In the center of the map, I describe God's prior activity while we are on the journey. First, God extends to each person a measure of prevenient grace. In chapter 2 on grace, I described what prevenient grace is and how this grace acts in our lives. Any recognition of God, and our need for God, is a result of this prior grace. We never start on the journey to God, or do anything that inclines us toward God, without it first being enabled and initiated by God's prevenient grace. God refuses to give up and continually provides and maintains a way—the King's Highway—back to God.

Also in the center of the map, I make a general line of demarcation between unawakened and awakened people. Again, do not focus on a precise sequence. Instead, look for vital signs of a person's awareness and interest in God and the sin in her life. As a relational discipler, we should be on the constant lookout for those who are being awakened and then immediately invite them to join a class meeting. This guide of the woods can be used as a tool to help identify and lookout for awakened people.

Relational Discipleship

The second column addresses those things that we encounter along the journey that either helps or inhibits our journey back to God. In previous chapters, I have introduced hindrances to God's grace as barriers the church erects, blockages the world scatters along the highway, and baggage that individual travelers carry with them that interfere with grasping God's grace. These hindrances are highlighted in gray. In this same column, the means of grace remain in white, and they are things that both the relational discipler and disciple can do to help overcome and move beyond hindrances to God's grace.

There may be barriers, blockages, and baggage present that I have not suggested in this particular segment. Each person is unique and has different experiences. We need to be sensitive as we listen to the story of the disciple to begin to discern those things that block God's grace in the disciple's life.

The same also applies to varied means of grace. As we engage in relational discipleship, the Holy Spirit may guide the disciple into other means of grace unique to her location and experiences beyond the ones I indicate. The one clarification I will make about the means of grace is that I believe the instituted means of grace are not optional. Instituted means of grace are those means that Wesley believed Jesus instituted, and are vehicles of God's grace throughout the ages. However, how and when a disciple learns and develops a faithful practice of the instituted means of grace can and will vary.

It would be impossible to identify every potential hindrance and means of grace. There are as many hindrances and means of grace as there are people and moments. I can only name and discuss a few of these in each segment on the journey back to God's house. As for the means of grace, I will be limited to addressing the instituted means of grace mostly. I will attempt to describe other potential means of grace briefly as we move forward.

Just as with the steps on the journey, we must not look at where I have located particular hindrances and means of grace on the journey. A person may not be troubled by any of the hindrances listed in this particular segment. We must again be sensitive to the Holy Spirit and the story of the traveler as they confess it to us. I will add, because of formational importance, I do think that the instituted means of grace should be close to where I locate them on the journey, but again flexibility and development should always be of concern.

The Unawakened

As we attempt to consider the qualities of the unawakened condition, it would be helpful first to understand the causes of an unawakened state. Everyone has experienced an unawakened state to some degree. Some people may have been raised in a church where they have always had some degree of awareness of God. Others may have been raised in a worldly context where God and sin were never addressed. Regardless, scripture points to the fact that we have all entered this world and live in this unawakened state for at least some period of time (Romans 3:23, Colossians 1:21). As we are awakened to God and sin, most of us can recognize a time where we were either unaware of God or at least did not have a meaningful interest in God.

As an orthodox Christian from a Wesleyan tradition, I view this unawakened state through the lens of original sin. Recently, there has been discussion about the character of original sin.[3] Again, my concern is not to exhaustively address this current theological discussion.[4] Regardless of how we want to describe original sin, I assert that the unawakened state is either the result of or a depiction of original sin. I appreciate Greg Boyd's approach to original sin and our alienation.[5] He asserts that our initial self-imposed alienation from God and others results in the unawakened state we experience.[6]

This self-imposed alienation originated in us wanting to be like God in ways that God did not intend.[7] The self-imposed alienation is first recorded in the story of the Garden of Eden, when the serpent told Eve, "you will be like God" (Gen. 3:4–5).God desired for us to be like God in the way God loves.[8] However, that was not sufficient for us. We wanted to judge as God judges. This judging resulted in us judging God, others, and ourselves. The power to judge also created the fear of being judged. With the fear of being judged, alienation occurred, and we began to hide ourselves from God and others. I am confident that there is not a single person who has

---

3. One example of the discussion around original sin can be found with the writings of Roger Wolsey. "A Progressive Christian View of Sin and Sinners."

4. We also often overlook the "original good" found in the Genesis account. "God saw that it was good" (Genesis 1).

5. Boyd, *Repenting*, 17.

6. Boyd, *Repenting*, 19.

7. Ibid., 35.

8. Ibid., 48.

lived a life free from the inclination to judge and the fear of being judged aside from Jesus Christ.

The unawakened person attempts to make the best of this condition. This person is unaware or uninterested that there is a Source to reconcile this alienation. There are many ways a person in this state attempts to deal with this disease of judging and of fearing judgment. My "Map of the Woods" attempts to give some conceptualization to this location. Some people try to ignore their spiritual state. They ignore those fears as they try to make life bearable by creating their own living space. However, they are always evaluating themselves against the lives of others. They are task or object oriented, always wanting more to "justify" who they are and what they do. Examples of this location would be materialism, consumerism, or a success orientation. We see much of this condition illustrated in the map of the woods as either steps or hindrances.

Other people in this location attempt to live carefree lives, not caring about anyone or anything else. They move from one experience to another, searching for the next experience that makes them feel "free." While there is some level of medicating this hunger of the soul, ultimately these people never find the satisfaction they so deeply crave. Often, they can be found wandering aimlessly outside the Source, which can provide the fulfillment they need. We might see examples of this living exhibited by alcoholism, drug addiction, sex addiction, and aimless wandering in life. Again, we can locate where this person is by referencing the map.

Other people fully embrace their harsh, judgmental condition. They are bitter, harsh, and mean-spirited. If they do believe in God, they shake their fists in God's face for not being the God that they believe God should be. Other people are objects to be used and abused. This condition results in people being their own gods, who judge and award sentences to others around them. People in this location might be spouse abusers, child abusers, or verbal abusers.

It is important that, while we see characteristics or actions that potentially help us locate people in this unawakened state, we do not identify people by their actions. Their actions are symptoms of their state and not who the people truly are. Our first obligation is to ascribe unsurpassable worth to everyone regardless of their location and symptoms. In our optimistic confidence in God's universal and always at work grace, we can be sure that even in the worst symptom or location that God is already on the scene as *the first responder*. God is initiating the rescue to bring the

The Woods

unawakened to spiritual consciousness and to begin the healing that is needed. We must join God in seeing the person as she was created to be and avoid the temptation to identify her by her symptoms.

We can identify some of the prevalent idols that are erected in people's lives which become barriers to God's grace. Many times, the idols we find people worshipping are wealth, sexuality, and knowledge.[9] Again, there are probably as many idols as there are people. In most instances, we can trace the idol back to one of these three. The unawakened person then erects walls around these idols to insulate this idol worship from God and other people.[10] This isolation results in broken relationships.[11] When people erect walls and create their own shacks in which to live, loneliness always results. In this world, all of us can identify both broken relationships we have experienced and witnessed in others. Broken relationships always hurt and leave deep wounds and scars.

My Wesleyan and Relational lens always interpret both sin and sins as a relational problem.[12] Relating poorly always interferes with and often causes broken relationships with God and others. When the church attempts to identify sins, plural, as the problem, the church is only treating the symptoms. The root of the problem is always sin, singular, or our experienced alienation from God. As relational disciplers, our first focus is on the alienation and not the sins.[13] When we focus on the sins (actions) of the unawakened first, we are creating a barrier to God's grace.

A perfect example of addressing the alienation first and being a means of grace is Jesus' approach to the woman at the well (John 4:1–42). Jesus' way of approaching and conversing with the woman created a safe place, where the woman felt at ease to confess her story. Obviously, Jesus was able to lead the woman from being unawakened to being awakened in one conversation. We should not feel compelled always to do the same. Restoring the bridge for a person to the King's highway may take time. Therefore, we do not treat symptoms first, or create a space where the person feels

---

9. Meeks, *Economist*, 21.

10. Ibid., 22.

11. Akkerman, Oord, Perterson, 70.

12. In chapter three on hospitality and chapter five on the degrees of faith, I describe the difference between sin (singular) as alienation and sins (plural) as actions. Sin is the condition, and sins are the manifestation.

13. There is an obvious need to address a sin that is immediately threatening the safety of the person or others.

like she has to hide her symptoms. As relational disciplers, we focus on the alienation first.

In describing the unawakened state, I have enumerated barriers, blockages, and baggage that interrupt or interfere with God's grace. People in an unawakened state have little to no awareness and interest in God and their sin condition, so God and the relational discipler have to do most of the heavy lifting for these people. There are little means of grace (spiritual disciplines) we can expect the unawakened to do. As relational disciplers, we are a means of grace to the unawakened.

An example of being a means of grace was Wesley's field preaching. Wesley utilized preaching to both awaken people and to identify those awakened. Once they were awakened, he would immediately enroll them in a society and class meeting.[14] He did not fret about those who were still unawakened. Yes, he preached to awaken them, but he did not invest his time in discipling them. his discipling effort was focused on people who were awakened and beginning the journey back to God.

I began this chapter with a classic hymn used in my tradition, *Make Me a Blessing*. The song urges us to be a blessing to those in the highways and byways of life. In a similar fashion, Jesus refers to people that follow Him as the "light of the world" (Matthew 5:14). Understanding the analogy of people awakening from sleep, we understand that vision is sensitive. Too bright of a light and the person winces. Relational disciplers must be sensitive to the light we provide to the awakening person. The light needs to be like a candle where the person can be attracted to the light. If we attempt to shine a spotlight, then the person will often hide from the light or be blinded. Our light should be a blessing to the disciple as they become awakened and not act like a hindrance to the process.

In the four stages of hospitality, the relational discipler focuses on the welcome of the unawakened person. To offer a hospitable biblical welcome, the relational discipler needs to focus on the key traits of hospitality that support this kind of welcome. One of the biggest obstacles to being awakened is the feeling of strangeness. A person will never feel free to open up and confess her journey until she no longer feels like a stranger. A relational discipler needs to offer a welcome that reduces this feeling of strangeness.

People are often awakened by crisis or traumatic moments in their lives. Death, marriage, the arrival of a baby, loss of a job, divorce, or any sudden life changes are places where people experience some awakening

---

14. J. Wesley, *The Works of John Wesley*, vol. 7, 207.

to God and their sin condition. It is at these moments we can display that holiness or perfect love I referenced in the cycle of transformation. Relational disciplers can listen, be present, encourage the disciple, cry with them, laugh with them, and offer support. Often, what the disciple really needs is someone simply to 'be' with them until they begin to recognize the presence of God that is constantly with them. It is these small acts of perfect love that attract people to want God and a similar change in their life. These acts are what enables God's grace to invite the smallest steps of repentance or to turn back toward God.

Relational discipleship can be both defined and expressed as a more helpful model of discipleship in its focus on overcoming perceived and experienced alienation, which fosters proper and healthy relationships with God and others. In the overview of this segment of the woods, I do not claim to depict all ways that people are unawakened or how they live in this state. Our responsibility is to look for the vital signs that indicate awareness or concern for God. In the unawakened state, relational disciplers are attempting to cooperate with God through biblical hospitality to help move a person from being unawakened to awakened. As soon as the discipler perceives an awakening, the awakened person should be included in a class meeting.

The Awakened

The awakened person is one who is showing signs of spiritual life and concern. When a person is awakened, the person no longer has only an awareness of God and her condition of life, but a desire to do something about this awareness. The holiness or perfect love that the traveler has experienced from God or the relational discipler has created a hunger in the traveler to display or experience this same love. As the traveler experiences the beauty of this holiness, remorse may swell up for the condition of her life, which will enable the traveler to begin to move forward.

Just as Abraham and the father of the prodigal stood at their doors watching for the traveler, the relational discipler is always on the lookout for signs of awakening. The smallest effort to begin the journey home to God should be celebrated and welcomed. The ever so small awareness of God should immediately get our attention. The slightest recognition of one's condition in life should give us hope, just like the sprout of life we witness at the very beginning of spring. It is not the responsibility of the traveler to make it to us—to either make the right decision, say the right words, or demonstrate a change of living. As relational disciplers, we run to, welcome, and restore the traveler before she even gets close to home. In our biblical hospitality, we are nudging those who are asleep to arise and come to life after their slumber. We are paying attention to the vital signs showing us where new life is beginning. This awakened person is showing an awareness and interest in God and/or awareness and concern about the sin in one's life.

As the relational discipler continually supports the disciple, there are a variety of barriers, blockages, and baggage that hinder the disciple receiving and responding to God's grace. The more one experiences spiritual transformation, the more responsible one can become in overcoming these hindrances. In the earlier stages, the relational discipler, with the help of the Holy Spirit, needs to take extra care in reducing these hindrances as much as possible. The means of grace are again the ways that hindrances can be moved, let go, overcome, and ways to lay hold of God's grace.

For the relational discipleship model to work, the relational discipler must be committed to restore the class meeting as a means of grace. Any awakened person should be encouraged to become a participating member of a class meeting. This activity should be one of the first means of grace that we teach and offer awakened people. It is the class meeting that provides the accountable small group where one can feel restored and safe. In this setting, people can experience what they need to give them the strength to confess the story of their journey. It is this means of grace that will provide the teaching and accountable practice of other means of grace where group members hold each other accountable for those practices.[15] This class meeting will provide opportunity for the testimony of others further up the highway on the journey back to God's house helping to clear the path and point the way forward for other travelers just beginning the journey.[16] Holy conferencing is one of the instituted means of grace I described in chapter 4 on the class meeting. The class meeting is a form of holy conferencing and must be considered essential and important at the very first signs of spiritual life.

---

15. See chapter four for a discussion on accountability in the class meeting.

16. John Wesley's *General Rules* are an important frame of reference for building the class meeting around. See J. Wesley, *The Works of John Wesley*, vol. 8, 255. Also see Kevin Watson's rewording of the *General Rules* for our time. Watson, *Blueprint*, 49–89.

The members of the class meeting will be able to hear and suggest other means of grace as each member confesses her story each week. Some members will share how a song conveyed God's grace at a particular time during the week. Another person may share how a friend stopped by and offered an encouraging word at just the right time. A class member may confess a divine appointment when she provided a meal and prayed with a stranger. In the class meeting, prayer will be modeled and shared as an essential means of grace. Members of the class, will over time, be able to share experiences where the Holy Spirit prompted a specific engagement. The class meeting should be our primary means of grace as a community to teach additional means of grace and help people up the highway to God's house.

Some Final Thoughts About the Woods

In the woods, the unawakened are either lost and wandering or attempting to live life in shacks created by their own efforts and ways of living. As God's grace goes out to the furthest point of alienation, God attempts to awaken those people who have little to no awareness of God and the condition of their lives. Relational disciplers cooperate with God's grace by being the means of grace to these unawakened people. The hospitality that is displayed by the relational disciplers will be essential in overcoming the feeling of strangeness. Works of mercy, like food, clothing, visiting, water, kindness, gentleness, and nonviolence performed by the relational disciplers will help to awaken people to a different way of living. Unawakened people will awaken to God and this perfect love displayed by the relational discipler through their outward actions and intercessory prayer. This action can generate a recognition of how this love is missing from their lives and will create a desire to want to experience and display this same love.

As people begin to show signs of awakening, the relational discipler will want to celebrate this new life and welcome the traveler into a class meeting. Again, the relational discipler must be the means of grace for these people. They will be incapable of seeing and understanding what the next steps are without the intentional care of the relational discipler. The relational discipler is providing safety and sanctuary to travelers who are wounded and tired. A constant lookout for barriers, blockages, and baggage must be primarily the responsibility of the relational discipler.

Relational Discipleship

The traveler will take small steps and then take a break. The traveler may even exhibit the cycle of resistance we explored in chapter 4 on the class meeting. It is natural for people to feel and demonstrate resistance and frustration as they experience God's grace disrupting their lives. Relational disciplers will offer the support and room for the disciple to work through this disruption. Even as the relational discipler patiently cares for the traveler, one must always keep the porch of God that is off in the distance in our sights and keep pointing the disciple in that direction.

7

The Porch

The story of the porch, told from the perspective of a traveler.

THE JOURNEY TO THIS legendary house was long and difficult. I am not sure how the events originally played out. However, after some time I woke up and recognized the destruction that I and others had brought to the world around me. I had lost friends and hurt members of my family. My life was shattered and torn apart. In my selfishness, I had only been worried about myself, but now I was becoming aware of others and what I had done to them.

As I awoke, I discovered that some very kind people ran to me and began to offer the help and resources I needed. At first, I was suspicious of their motives. From my perspective, they could not possibly have known what I had gone through or needed. They kept referring to this 'kind neighbor' who lived further up the highway from us and could provide me sanctuary. They urged me to make the journey to go and stay with this neighbor for a while.

All I could think of was what I would do with all the possessions I had stored in bags and boxes that I tried to rescue from the rubble of what still existed of my life. I certainly could not carry all this baggage to this neighbor's house. It would be too heavy of a burden to bear. Why should I make this journey? Why couldn't I just try to bring order back to my life? Who was this neighbor they kept talking about? Was this neighbor really as good and considerate as they were making him out to be?

Life was not getting any easier or better. I finally recognized that it was at least worth an attempt to visit this neighbor. These new friends recognized that I was finally ready to make the journey. What happened next was a total surprise to me. A group of these friends offered to make this journey with me. As we prepared for the journey, they recognized I was worried about all the baggage I had accumulated and what I would do with all of it. These friends took the time to sort through some of that baggage with me and listened to the stories surrounding this baggage. After contemplating the baggage that represented my life, I concluded that I could leave some of this baggage behind. I was surprised to discover that these people did not react adversely to the baggage that I refused to surrender, and they even offered to help me carry the baggage for the remainder of the journey.

We finally began the journey. These friends kept pointing to the neighbor's house off in the distance, further up the highway, but I could not make it out. I couldn't believe the kindness and welcome these friends showed me as we traveled. My new friends sensed I was beginning to grieve the loss of my old life, even though it had caused destruction. They patiently listened as I recalled stories from my past. They cried with me. At times, I thought for sure they would abandon me when I shared some very troubling things I had done. Throughout the confession of my life story, they remained by my side as we journeyed together toward the neighbor's house. They encouraged me as we traveled and reassured me that I would not regret making the journey.

Along the way, they were able to convince me to let go of more baggage, making the trip easier. It seemed as if they always were on the lookout for obstacles and distractions that could interfere with our trip. Occasionally, there were well-meaning acquaintances who would come to us on the journey and urge me to return, but my new friends were able to convince me to keep moving forward. Sometimes there were trees or big rocks blocking the way. These trees and rocks were often placed on the highway by people who still lived in the old community and were concerned with the number of people that were leaving. However, these good friends did all the heavy lifting to clear the path for me, knowing that I was still weak from the past destruction. Barriers were occasionally placed by acquaintances of my new friends that were concerned about new travelers damaging the highway or scandalizing the neighbor's house. My friends would lovingly encourage these people to stop blocking the way and instead help the weak and injured travelers make their way to the neighbor's house.

I could finally see the porch of the house. There were many people who were on the porch, yet there was still room for more. I could tell that all these people on the porch were tired and injured from their journey from

The Porch

their previous life to the neighbor's porch. It was on this porch that my fellow travelers had found rest, nourishment, and healing. I was surprised to find that there were much more of these new friends who welcomed, provided hospitality and answered the questions of the travelers. I approached the steps of the porch. Exhausted, I could not find the strength to make it up these steps. I almost collapsed, but as I did many of these friends came to me, supported me, and helped me to find a place on the porch.

As I sat on the porch, I found myself asking all sorts of questions. Why did I not know this neighbor before? Can I trust this neighbor? Can this neighbor help all the people I see coming and resting on this porch? Why did my new friends care for me so much? What is this neighbor like? Will I meet this neighbor? Has this neighbor been here all along?

I also wonder, is there a chance I could become like these new friends of mine? I found myself wanting to be like my new friends. For so long, I had thought only of myself and caused so much pain and suffering in the lives of others that I wondered if there was hope that I could serve others like my new friends did. These new friends patiently and lovingly listened to my concerns and questions and answered as they best could.

Then it happened! I caught a glimpse of who I perceived to be the neighbor. The neighbor went from person to person, and he took the time to embrace people. He wiped tears away from crying children and spent time answering the questions that people had for the neighbor. I listened and absorbed every touch, every movement, and every word this neighbor said and did. Then the neighbor came to me. The neighbor knew my hesitation and recognized my questions and baggage. I found out that the neighbor was patient with me, not rushing any movement or conclusions.

Over the several days that I had been on the porch, I had witnessed some people leaving the porch. I noticed that the neighbor and new friends would urge these people to stay, but they would never force or block people from leaving the porch. In fact, as people did leave the porch, I witnessed the neighbor sobbing as he watched them walk off in the distance. I could not figure out why this neighbor cared so much for these strangers.

Over the course of the couple days that I have been on the porch, I saw the neighbor invite people inside his house. I marveled at the big, beautiful door and wondered why it was always left open. What was interesting was that the neighbor always left the door open. I could not understand why the neighbor left the door open when so many strangers were resting just outside the entrance on the porch. I began to become suspicious of the neighbor and his intentions again. Although my suspicions were raised, I was drawn to the open door, curious about what was on the other side. My imagination ran wild as I fantasized about what the other side of this open door would reveal. However, every time one of these guests agreed to come into the house, I was confused by the combination of laughter and crying that I heard. Many people would often just stand in the doorway for long periods of time.

My turn finally came. One evening, while the neighbor and I were having a conversation with some of my new friends, the neighbor invited me into his house. I had grown more comfortable with my new friends and the neighbor, but as the neighbor's invitation to enter into his house lingered in the air, I could feel a sense of terror and anxiety that words cannot effectively describe rising up in me. I had been so deeply wounded by people that I had put my trust in, and I was not ready to trust this new neighbor that I had just met. I was worried that the neighbor would be offended as I rejected his invitation. However, his response left me astounded. The neighbor simply agreed and changed the conversation. I have never seen this neighbor force or argue with anyone. The neighbor simply opened his home and offered hospitality to everyone who chose to seek refuge on his porch. The neighbor and his friends ensured that people had access to whatever they needed as they wrestled with the decision to enter into the neighbor's house or to return to the old community.

I pondered the neighbor's offer to enter into his home. I recalled his gentle nature, the sound of his voice, the love in his eyes. I had not experienced a loving gaze like that before. Every once in a while, the neighbor would ask again. My new friends would talk about their experience of going into the neighbor's house. The neighbor would talk about how his son was the one who masterfully crafted the door and made it possible for anyone to enter into the house. The neighbor and his friends continued to converse with me on the porch, reminding me of the life that I had left behind and the healing that had already taken place as I sought refuge on the neighbor's porch. As we conversed, I began to sense a deeper need for healing as they gently urged me to come into the neighbor's house. Finally, I regained enough strength and had enough trust in the neighbor to accept the neighbor's invitation to enter the house. I began to make my way around the porch and proceeded to approach the door. What would I find? What will I see? Will I experience the crying and laughter that others who have gone before me experienced? I stood just before the door ready to enter . . .

The Porch	The King's Highway — Convincing Grace	God's Action	Location — Resting and Learning Who God is on the Porch	
	Works of Mercy - Feeding, Clothing, Visiting			Approaches the Door
	Overly focused on non-essentials			Senses God cares for personal condition
	Partisanship			Longs to be Known and Loved by God
	Over Sexualized Society			Aware of Cost
	Unforgiving Spirit			Receptive to spiritual advice
	Rejection			Ability to confess one's story
	Competition			More aware of God's grace each week
	Emphasizing Strangeness			More regular in attention to means of grace
	Searching Scriptures			Increasing hunger for the things of God
	Legalism			Aware of different way of being as a Christian
	Low Self Esteem			Gratitude Beginning
	Worship			Positive attitude toward Gospel
	Doubts			Grasp implications of Gospel
	Sins			Aware of personal need
	Mental Aptitudes			Aware of Basics of Gospel
	Prayer			Interested in Jesus
	Class Meeting			Wonders if God can be known
	Potential Blockages, Barriers, and Baggage and the Means of Grace to Move Barriers			Steps to the House of God

(shaded)	= Barriers, Blockages, and Baggage
(unshaded)	= Means of Grace

Analysis of the Map

From the previous story and the map of the porch (figure 9), we get an idea of what the traveler experiences while on the porch. It is essential to remember that people will experience the journey, possible hindrances, and various means of grace in their own individual ways. There is not a specific formula that can be applied to every person on this journey to indicate the variety, order, and timing that these various experiences will occur. However, every person that accepts the call to travel on this journey will experience these things at some point on their journey. The map is only to give the relational discipler a general way of locating the disciple and ascertaining the needed direction to encourage the disciple forward. The arrangement of the map matches the form and flow of the previous map of the woods.

In each location highlighted on the map, we recognize God's grace is always initiating the response of the traveler to continue on the journey. In this particular location on the porch, we find God's prevenient grace acting as convincing grace. This grace always acts prior to any action the disciple takes toward God and God's house. God's prevenient grace is in action long before the traveler makes any decision to go on the journey toward the neighbor's porch and enter into his home. This grace is working to convince the traveler that there is hope to redeem her prior life, ways, and activities. This grace is also convincing the traveler that God is the source of this redeeming action. Convincing grace is never forceful or coercive. It is always optimistic, universal, but at times overwhelming.

In this convincing grace, people can be overwhelmed by having to recognize and confess their previous story and location. This convincing grace reveals the perfect love that God is and is modeled by the relational disciplers when they join travelers on the journey toward the neighbor's house. It is common for travelers to experience a sense of being overwhelmed by the kindness and gentleness of their new friends who join them on their journey, which is also modeled by the neighbor as God invites them to enter into God's house. This awareness can increase discomfort as the travelers recognize the significant difference between the love and hospitality they experience on their journey and on God's porch and that which was experienced in the old community. It is the hope and prayer of the neighbor and the disciplers that this perfect love will convince the travelers of their need to experience this perfect love while planting seeds of desire to reciprocate this love to others.

This perfect love is demonstrated by the unending hospitality. While the travelers were journeying through the woods, the hospitality focused on the welcome and reduced sense of strangeness. When the travelers took refuge on the neighbor's porch, hospitality was present in the form of restoration. The travelers experienced a meaningful welcome when they arrived at the neighbor's porch, but restoration was the central focus of the hospitality being lavished on these weary travelers. The relational discipler must focus on the key traits of hospitality that prepare the travelers to experience the needed restoration that results from the confession of their story as they begin to find the healing and rest that is needed after completing such an exhausting journey.

The key traits that aid in this restoration will continue to incorporate the key traits practiced in the woods, but will now add more depth. Those key traits included gift-giving and generosity, risk-taking, and reducing strangeness. Safety and promise keeping will be essential for the traveler to experience restoration on the porch. These key traits should be clearly practiced in the class meeting. As I have explained, the awakened person should become part of the class meeting at the moment she is awakened to God. Thus, ideally, the awakened person would have joined a class meeting while she was still located in the woods. The relational discipler will need to demonstrate continually that the class meeting is a safe place for the traveler as she moves onto the porch. The traveler should not fear ridicule, rejection, attacks, or judgment. A safe environment is created as the traveler recognizes the practical demonstration of promise keeping.[1] The relational discipler must be intentional to be both faithful in word and action to the traveler. The purpose of promise-keeping is to generate confidence that the relational discipler is reliable, genuine, and can be trusted to continue the journey with the traveler into the neighbor's house.

The relational discipler will have to be on the lookout for potential hindrances that prohibit or inhibit the traveler from recognizing or responding to God's grace. Again, I have enumerated potential hindrances on the map. Hindrances may be morally neutral but still interfere with the traveler's ability to grasp and respond to God's grace. The church unfortunately still creates barriers that keep the travelers from resting on the porch

---

1. Again, promise keeping and the other key traits were discussed in chapter three on hospitality.

and finding the restoration the traveler needs to move on in God's house. The world will, through temptations, lies, and distractions, attempt to block a traveler from responding to the grace of God. Finally, the relational discipler must understand that the traveler will continue to carry baggage from past experiences and other factors that interfere with God's grace.

As the relational discipler approaches these hindrances, the relational discipler will engage in means of grace on behalf of the disciple to help remove these obstacles. Also, the relational discipler will further teach the traveler the accountable practice of the means of grace. By accountable practice, I mean that the disciple will report to the class meeting each week about the practice and experiences surrounding the means of grace. On the porch, the traveler should be engaging and becoming more comfortable in the class meeting as a means of grace. Additionally, the relational discipler should begin to model, teach, and hold the traveler accountable for the practice of prayer as a means of grace. As the relational discipler witnesses growth and the accountable practice of prayer, then the discipler should model, teach, and hold the traveler accountable for attendance at a worship service at least once a week. As the traveler progresses on her journey, searching the scriptures will be added as a means of grace to faithfully practice and engage in.

As we explore each map, we will recognize the primacy of the means of grace. These means of grace are how we locate the disciple, offer hospitality, remove hindrances, and help the disciple move forward. The relational discipler will always engage the means of grace on behalf of the disciple, but in each progressive map, the disciple will increasingly engage the means of grace on her own.

Cookie cutter experiences and our own notion of time should not dictate the implementation and practice of the means of grace. We should expect slow and uneven transformation. The traveler will not always be faithful in the practice of the means of grace. The relational discipler should communicate that it is expected that the traveler will not always be faithful in the practice of the means of grace. However, the discipler should communicate that God is always faithful regardless of our faithfulness. With God always being faithful, in our failure to faithfully practice the means of grace we simply confess our unfaithfulness and resume engagement with the means of grace. The relational discipler gives room for unfaithfulness so that the traveler feels safe confessing her failure. If we make the means of grace about how faithfully we practice them, then we create a barrier to

God's grace by making the means of grace the end and not the means. In this improper view, we communicate that the means of grace are a work of salvation rather than a work of transformation. The relational discipler must keep a proper awareness and practice of the means of grace for the disciple by how the means of grace are communicated and reported in the class meeting.

As the relational discipler keeps a pulse on the spiritual life of the traveler on the porch, other means of grace may be suggested as the traveler confesses other hindrances being experienced. Maybe the traveler needs a particular works of mercy to help her with a particular piece of baggage she is carrying (i.e. health care, shelter, or food). Perhaps the traveler needs some additional one-to-one discipling. Another suggestion might be that the traveler needs to listen to some worship music during the week to help feed her soul. Since the traveler may be new to Bible reading, perhaps the traveler requires some practical guidance on Bible study and how to search the scriptures devotionally. The class meeting is the place where relational disciplers listen closely to the story the traveler is confessing on the porch in order to cooperate with the restorative work God is already doing.

When the relational discipler recognizes that a traveler is on the porch and is beginning to experience restoration, then the relational discipler can begin sharing about what the Son—Jesus has done to create and open the door to God's house. The relational discipler can begin to share her personal experience of walking through that door. As the relational discipler continues to share her stories, she will continue to listen to the story of the traveler. The Holy Spirit will prompt the appropriate time to invite the traveler through the door of God's house. It is important for the relational discipler to refrain from coercing, forcing, or pushing the traveler to go through the door. The relational discipler can invite and willingly accept the answer of the traveler. If it is not accepted the first time, then the relational discipler continues to engage the means of grace accountably until it is time for the next invitation. Then, the relational discipler can lovingly extend the invitation to the traveler in the confidence that God—the neighbor—has been working to convince the traveler, through the means of grace, to enter the house.

Again, we recognize the cycle of resistance as a real and probable cycle that each traveler will experience to some degree as she sits on the porch and experiences God's convincing grace. God's convincing grace can be disturbing as the traveler recognizes the difference between her old life and this new way of living being demonstrated by God and the relational disciplers. The relational discipler must give room for the traveler to express and experience that rage from the felt discontentment. We cannot prematurely direct or force people through this cycle. As the traveler sits on the porch and experiences the safety and faithfulness we exhibit, in time, the rage will turn into grief as she comes to terms with God's convincing grace. As relational disciplers, we should grieve with them. We grieve with them as they turn away and leave certain baggage behind. Finally, light will begin to break forth in the darkness as they recognize the goodness and potential for God's grace. As praise and gratitude swell up within the traveler, the relational discipler can join them on the journey toward the door of God's house. This cycle could occur several times while a traveler rests on the porch of God. It all depends on how much baggage the traveler has brought with them.

As people go through this cycle of resistance and we recognize the people entering the final stage of praise and gratitude, then we become aware of the effectiveness of the means of grace in their lives. This gratitude is the second step of the cycle of experiencing God's grace. The experience of God's grace is the first step. Then, as a person comes to terms with and openly receives God's grace, the response will always be gratitude. Gratitude is how we know a person is open to and responding to God's grace positively. People cannot respond to God's grace positively without welling up with gratitude. Finally, a person that wells up with gratitude will want to gift or share that same grace. We will witness these travelers sharing with others outside the class meeting what grace they are experiencing, and they will share within the class meeting what God is doing. As the traveler and the other class meeting participants begin to respond positively to God's grace, new life begins to blossom within their lives.

Prayerfully, there will come a time where the traveler has experienced enough restoration and demonstration of perfect love that she will respond positively to the invitation to walk through the door of God's house. The means of grace that the traveler has engaged in up to this point will serve as the catalyst for spiritual growth and transformation to form a foundation for understanding and experiencing what God is doing in her life. In the other models of discipling that I described in the Introduction, none of this discipling would have occurred yet. These other models would have instead focused first on getting the person to say a sinner's prayer. Then, these other models potentially would have invited the "newly saved" person to enter some form of discipleship. These models operate without the careful cultivation and recognition of God's grace that the relational discipleship model affords at the earliest signs of being awakened. In the relational discipleship model, the relational discipler engages in intentional discipleship with the traveler and begins this process prior to justification. This prior discipleship optimizes God's prevenient grace, which is already working in the life of the traveler, and recognizes that the harvest truly is plentiful. We now find the disciple at the door of God's house, ready to experience the reality that she has been the child of God all along.

8

The Door

The story of the door, told from the perspective of a traveler.

As I approached the door, I had reservations as the fear and doubt that was flooding my mind began to affect my breathing and my heart rate. What was I thinking? Do I really need to enter the house for more healing? After all, I was doing a lot better. I barely know these new friends of mine and was still getting to know this neighbor. Their love seems almost too perfect—too good to be true. I have never seen anyone from my old world love like this. I kept inching toward the door—step after step.

I could see the door, which always stood open, and it had a simple, yet intriguing design. The wood was rough and the nails large and rusty, but somehow this old rugged design had some level of deeper allure to it. I had often heard the neighbor tell me the story of how the neighbor's son made this door possible. Now, I saw firsthand how much love and detail went into this door. I could sense the blood, sweat, and tears that the son put into this door. It really did make the house more inviting.

What surprised me was that I had not yet met the neighbor's son. As I moved closer, a person in front of me walked through the door. I could see someone reach out and greet this person from the shadow of the door. I couldn't quite make the person out, but there was something similar in the gestures and movement that I recognized from somewhere else. As I moved one step closer, it dawned on me that it was very similar—almost identical—to how I have seen this neighbor act. Could this be the neighbor's son?

I became even more anxious as my next step would be through this door, and I would see who this person was.

A couple of my new friends helped me to the door. They understood my fears, doubts, and worries because they had at one time experienced them as well. As we waited for my turn to enter the door of the neighbor's house, we continued to confess and share our stories. We shared from where we had come and what we had experienced. They, again, talked about this neighbor and son and of their first time walking through the door. I hadn't noticed until now that, through all the confession of our stories that I had been able to lay down some more of the baggage I had brought with me. My burden was feeling even lighter.

Before I stepped through the door, I finally began to discern what was inside the house. It looked like there was a big party or feast going on inside. People were full of life and joy. I couldn't believe how the neighbor was able to be almost everywhere at one time. I would see the neighbor interacting with some people in one area and then the very next moment I would notice him over in the other corner greeting other people. This neighbor's hospitality continued to amaze me.

Then, I caught a glimpse of a picture hanging on the wall above the fireplace, directly across from the door where I was standing. Could it be? All of a sudden, I was flooded with an emotion which I couldn't explain. The picture that I saw looked a lot like me as a child with this neighbor. How could this be?

I never knew my father growing up. My mother never really talked about my father. There was always a hole in my heart longing to know something about him. I would often wonder if my father was thinking of me. Did my father love me? Was I like my father? Where was my father? Why did I never know who my father was? As I saw this picture, somehow deep inside it felt like I knew this neighbor was my father. I looked closer and saw an older child with this neighbor and me. Was this a brother I never knew I had? Now, I was hungry, even desperate, to get inside this house and find the answers to my questions.

The moment was finally here. My new friends approached the door with me and personally introduced me to the person greeting in the shadow of the door. They reached out and said, "We would like you to meet the neighbor's son." The son reached out to me and drew me in closely with an embrace that only an older brother could give. In this embrace, I felt like I had finally come home from being lost. A joy that I never had flooded my soul. A peace that can only come from coming back home rested on me. I knew for sure that this neighbor was my father, and this son was my brother.

I couldn't move. I had to stand in this doorway for some time. The son talked with me at great lengths. These new friends stood with me and helped me to adjust to this new life. They continued to support me and helped bear some of the remaining baggage I was still carrying. Questions were being answered. Stories of my father and brother were being shared. I was learning who they were and who I am now. As we continued to talk, my father made his way to me. We embraced like never before. At this moment, I could recognize why this neighbor extended the hospitality he did. It is the love of a father for his children.

After some time, my father offered an invitation for me to come and see the house with him. He also invited me to move home with him—to live in his house as a permanent resident, not as a visitor. I was still trying to make sense of it all and didn't accept the invitation quite yet. I still had some baggage that I was concerned wouldn't fit well in my father's house. There was a part of me that was homesick for the old community. Yes, I was thrilled to be his child, but all of this change was just too much. My father recognized my reluctance and just encouraged me to consider his offer. He urged me to stay in the doorway as long as I needed. My new friends, brother, and father kept encouraging and listening to me.

My new friends also shared how they, like me, wrestled with moving back home with our father. I guess it took some time for me to realize these friends were also my family. They indicated it took some time for them to reconcile their confusion and mixed feelings as well. These family members even shared some ways they arrived at their decision.

As we waited together at the door, they made sure I had food. They would regularly provide some bread and wine and the father and son came and joined us during this time. This time was a special time of celebration and communion. I cherished this time as it seemed to not only feed me physically but somehow fed my soul as well.

The father with the help of his children composed a family book that explained the story of the family. These family members read it with me. Often the father would stop by during these readings and add a unique perspective that somehow always connected to me personally. I was learning about this father and brother, and the extent they went to create this house and bring the family back home.

The Door

Over time, all the obstacles hindering my moving back home with the father were removed. As I laid aside more baggage, I grew closer to my new family. I began to have a deeper love for my father, brother, and family. In my growing awareness, I even began to help with some chores around the house. I would go out onto the porch and help feed and care for other tired, hungry and wounded travelers. Taking time for these travelers, I began to hear their stories about coming to the porch. I found myself sharing my experience with them. It was becoming clearer to me that I truly wanted to live permanently with my father in this house and join his mission.

Analysis of the Map

As we reflect on the story and the "map of the door," this would be an appropriate place to review the cycle of transformation I described in chapter 4 on the class meeting. I took the three doctrines Wesley thought to be foundational to Methodism and described them as a cycle of transformation we repeatedly experience. A person first experiences God's holiness or perfect love. As a person recognizes this wholly other way of being, the person begins to recognize how her life and ways of being do not conform to this perfect love. In this recognition, the person wants to draw toward that love and reflect that love. We define this process as repentance. God recognizes the slightest indications that the traveler is receptive to God's love, and as the traveler begins to turn toward God, God runs toward the person. By God coming to the person, God enables the faith that this person can make the journey toward that perfect love and walks alongside the person. Our spiritual formation is made up of this continual cycle—holiness experienced, repentance, faith, and holiness lived out.

This cycle also demonstrates the larger journey back to God's house. In the woods, the lost traveler is awakened by the perfect love of God. The relational disciplers exhibit love through gracious hospitality. This love invites the traveler to recognize her need to move toward and reflect that same love. The traveler begins the journey home. At the very moment that the traveler makes the decision to begin the journey, repentance has begun. God and the relational disciplers run toward the awakened person and come alongside them to make the journey together in the class meeting. Through grace and the means of grace, the traveler's faith is enabled and strengthened. The traveler, with the help of the relational disciplers, makes it to the porch and sees perfect love even more clearly.

The Door	Potential Blockages, Barriers, and Baggage and the Means of Grace to Move Barriers	The King's Highway / Justifying Grace	God's Action	Location	Steps to the House of God
	Works of Mercy - Feeding, Clothing, Visiting				Recognizes a Need to Move In and Live with God
	Grief				Longs to Know God More
	Broken Relationships				Desire to Love God and Others More
	Sin				Recognizes a Deeper Love from God and Others
	Baptism				Hunger to Learn More About God
	Individualism				Becomes Active in the Body of Christ
	Poor Views of Atonement				Recognizes Areas of Life Needs Transformation
	Practical Atheism				Begins to Share the Gift of Grace Experienced
	Searching Scriptures				Begins to Live as a Child of God
	Abuse				Awarness of the Family of God
	Temptations				Inner Awareness of the Love of God
	Worship				Recognizes Place as a Child of God
	Pride				Gratitude Wells Up
	Eucharist				Experiences Forgiveness
	Addictions				Takes a Step of Faith to Walk through the Door
	Prayer				Ready to Leave Old Life Behind
	Class Meeting				At the Door

Walking through the door and seeing that I have been a child of God all along.

	= Barriers, Blockages, and Baggage
	= Means of Grace

THE DOOR

The door is the next step. In this step, we often think that repentance precedes and is needed for justifying grace. Wesley recognized that only minimal repentance is needed for God's justifying grace to be gifted and experienced in a person's life.[1] Greater experiences of repentance actually occur after justification.[2] We must recognize that full repentance is produced by God's Spirit even after one's redemption, or we make salvation works oriented. My proposed cycle of transformation helps us understand salvation as a gift, and our responses as enabled by God's grace. Before one moves onto justification, God's love is what invites one to respond or to repent.

Wesley understood the door of God's house to be Jesus Christ, and the work Jesus accomplished through his life, death, and resurrection. Many have suggested that one is not a child of God until she experiences justification.[3] I believe that view shortchanges God's love for all people and Christ's complete and universal work on the cross (Colossians 1:21). The position I have taken throughout this resource has emphasized that all people are the children of God—even prior to justification. Our self-imposed alienation is what separated us from God. This alienation made us judge God, and act in ways that made God a perceived enemy. If Jesus instructs us to love our enemies, then God will not do any less. God loved people, even while they acted like God's enemies and not God's children.

Christ's suffering and death were the distance God was willing to go to prove that we were still God's children. As one metaphorically approaches the door of God's house, a minimal degree of repentance is needed. There was a lot of blood, sweat, tears, love, and grace through Jesus Christ that went into God drawing each person to approach the door. While we can argue about the actual order of events, I propose that while a person is standing in front of the door she is beginning to recognize and experience the truth that she has always been a child of God. It is this experience of perfect love (*holiness*) that invites one to walk finally through (a degree of *repentance*) the door of justification. It is Christ's work through his life, death, and resurrection that enables the *faith* to walk through that door. Then, one is able fully to recognize and accept her place as a child of God (a degree of *holiness*).

1. J. Wesley, *The Works of John Wesley*, vol. 5, 58. Also see, J. Wesley, *The Works of John Wesley*, vol. 5, 81. Another good reference, J. Wesley, *The Works of John Wesley*, vol. 5, 253. Also Manskar, *Accountable*, 72.

2. J. Wesley, *The Works of John Wesley*, vol. 5, 156.

3. Watson, *Foreclose*, 12. Also see Watson's treatment of Gnosticism, Watson, *Foreclose*, 32. Also Watson, *Foreclose*, 93.

Relational Discipleship

Most travelers will spend some time in the doorway of God's house. It takes some time for people to embrace and live in this new reality of being a child of God. Unfortunately, some people will even walk back out the door and onto the porch and even potentially back into a lost state in the woods. Wesley could not understand how so many Christians will live in the door of God's house or even step back into their former ways of living.[4] He thought Methodism was uniquely equipped to help people to move all the way into God's house—to live in scriptural holiness.[5] This emphasis was what fueled Wesley's use of small accountability groups.[6] He recognized the likelihood that a person would move back into old ways of living without the means of grace experienced in small accountability groups.[7]

The map of the door (figure 10) follows the same layout as the previous two locations on the journey back to God's house. Like the other maps, the steps, hindrances, and means of grace are meant to be guidelines. The map again is a way for the relational discipler to find or "generally" locate and help support the disciple on the way forward. Relational discipling requires a constant listening to the story of the new disciple and discerning how the Holy Spirit is already present and at work. This practice of listening will also enable the relational discipler to be aware of barriers, blockages, and baggage that could inhibit the disciple from recognizing and responding to God's grace in a positive way.

Hospitality continues to be of primary importance for the relational discipler to extend and foster accountable discipleship. The relational discipler never ceases to provide the previous stages of hospitality to the traveler. Instead, the relational discipler builds upon the previous stages of hospitality. In this location of God's house, the relational discipler must continue to build upon the welcoming and restorative work begun in the previous locations. However, at the door, the relational discipler is now accompanying the traveler into a place where they dwell together. This place is where the mundane and messiness of discipleship often occurs. Hopefully, familiarity and a healthy level of comfort increases.

---

4. J. Wesley, *The Works of John Wesley*, vol. 11, 366. J. Wesley, Also see, *The Works of John Wesley*, vol. 5, 156. Also see, J. Wesley, *The Works of John Wesley*, vol. 6, 511.

5. J. Wesley, *The Works of John Wesley*, vol. 13, 9.

6. J. Wesley, *The Works of John Wesley*, vol. 1, 178. Also see, J. Wesley, *The Works of John Wesley*, vol. 8, 269.

7. J. Wesley, *The Works of John Wesley*, vol. 8, 252. Also see, J. Wesley, *The Works of John Wesley*, vol. 3, 144.

The Door

While the relational discipler may be anxious for the traveler to experience a crisis moment of justifying grace, patience and doing life together must be the priority. If the emphasis is placed on the immediacy of experiencing justifying grace, then the relational discipler creates a barrier where the traveler considers that the formula, not her own spiritual growth, is the true concern. Hospitality, that emphasizes a willingness to accept the traveler just as she is, gives the traveler the confidence to come to terms and wrestle with the grace God is extending.

Again, in this stage of hospitality, the relational discipler continues to exhibit the previous key traits of hospitality (defined in chapter 3 on hospitality) extended in the prior locations. Gift giving and generosity, risk taking, reducing strangeness, creating a safe environment, and promise keeping all continue to be features of this location. However, as the relationship has grown, the key traits of friendship and gratitude are added. Gratitude should have always been in some measure practiced. However, as deeper friendship increases, gratitude becomes more genuine. Every small step toward the house of God should be celebrated and gratitude expressed to both God and the traveler.[8]

This friendship requires quality time and a sense of enjoying the presence of the friend. As the relational discipler walks alongside the traveler to the door, and through the door, the relational discipler spends more time with the traveler. During this extended time, stories are shared, questions answered, and doubts and fears discussed.

As the relational discipler continues to listen to the confessed story of the traveler, the discipler can engage in the means of grace on the traveler's behalf. The discipler can pray for, fast for, and provide various works of mercy to lighten the traveler's load and to help overcome the potential barriers, blockages, and baggage that hinders interaction with God's grace.

The relational discipler will continue to help the traveler engage in the accountable practice of the means of grace taught in the previous locations. The means of grace, such as the class meeting, prayer, worship, and searching the scriptures will continue to be developed in this location. Additional means of grace, the sacraments of the Eucharist and Baptism, are now introduced. The relational discipler will be responsible for teaching the sacramental importance these two means of grace have in the life of the traveler.

One might notice from the map that in each subsequent location on the journey back to God's house how the means of grace, which are in white are

8. Oden, *Gospel*, 112.

increasing, while the hindrances to grace in the gray are decreasing. I believe there is a correlation to how we open ourselves to God's grace, and the impact hindrances can have on our ability to recognize and respond to God's grace. I do not suggest that life becomes easier for those more faithfully practicing the means of grace. However, I would suggest that the more we faithfully practice more means of grace, the more obstacles to God's grace will be overcome.

A relational discipler must always remember that transformation is slow and uneven. Just because a traveler enters the door of justifying grace does not mean the traveler will no longer experience the cycle of resistance. I do believe the more we experience transformation that this cycle of resistance will not always be a significant experience of resisting God's grace. Yet, there is always a process of coming to terms with God's further invitation. We will always feel a level of discontent as God's grace challenges our current lives. Hopefully, the more we are transformed, the less pronounced that cycle of resistance will occur.

At the door, as a traveler adjusts to this justifying grace, God will come along and offer the next invitation. For this location, that invitation is for the traveler to move all the way into God's house. God does not coerce the traveler to accept the invitation immediately. God gives room for the traveler to wrestle with the discontentment of leaving her old life and immersing herself in this new way of living. The traveler has to come to terms with the house chores and house rules. More baggage will have to be abandoned. The traveler is wrestling with living her life continually in the presence of God. The relational discipler remains faithful to the traveler and gives space for the traveler to reflect on this change.

As the means of grace are faithfully practiced, prayerfully over time, the traveler will come to terms with this feeling of discontent. It will morph into grief. The relational discipler comes alongside and grieves with the traveler as she mourns the loss of her old way of being and some more baggage she is willing to abandon.[9] In the class meeting, confession, support, and mutual burden bearing are essential. The discipler and disciple confess their stories of their struggles and decisions to move all the way home with God.

---

9. While there is celebration in abandoning our sin and old ways of living, in this segment I am emphasizing the cycle of resistance that I explained in chapter four on the class meeting. This cycle of resistance is experienced at some level every time we become aware of God's grace inviting us forward. We have to recognize our need and that our lives will change. The rage or discontent and the grief may not be as pronounced with every step but are certainly a proper process of weighing the cost (Luke 14:25–34).

The Door

Gradually, the traveler will prayerfully well up with gratitude and praise as she accepts the next invitation—the gift of living with God in God's house, a place where she can experience and receive God's gift of sanctifying grace. This traveler has recognized that every time she has been in the presence of God, she has experienced God's perfect love. This perfect love has changed her each time she experienced it. She understands that as she lives in the presence of this perfect love she will be continually transformed and grow. She desires to reflect and extend this perfect love that she has experienced. She is now ready to move into God's house of holiness.

9

The House

The story of the house, told from the perspective of a traveler.

It really was a big decision to move back home with my father and his family. After all, my life would never be the same. In my father's house, life would be very different. I was not sure all my baggage would be accepted. Would I be accepted? Was there room for me and all my baggage? Would the family be patient with me as I learned the new ways the family lived? Was I ready to surrender those things that were incompatible with living in this house? Was I willing to truly love the way I saw my father and other family members love one another? These questions and more flooded my thoughts as I weighed the cost of moving home.

    My father, older brother, and other family members were very patient with me. As I mentioned before, they allowed me to stay close to the door. They even allowed me to help with as many of the household chores as I was able. My family would frequently visit with me and share how they originally wrestled with their own decision to move back home. They confessed their experiences and how the process of addressing their doubts and fears took time to work through. During this time, I recognized how gentle my father really was. He made sure I knew I was welcome, and he would often lovingly invite me to move back home. However, in his invitation, I sensed that my father was not forcing a decision. He expressed a longing to heal the alienation I had experienced, and he was willing to let me work through my decision.

The House

Over time, I had witnessed, experienced, learned, and wrestled with what it meant to move back home. The time finally came for me to make the decision to commit to living with my father and family and accept what such a commitment involved. I asked a couple of close family members to go with me as I conveyed this news to our father. This decision was so important that I wanted to be supported as I shared my decision. I felt fear, happiness, sadness, worry and anxiety all wrapped up tightly within me as I came up to my father. As always, he was happy to see me and embraced me in such a way that I knew I was deeply loved.

He recognized there was something different about me this time. Again, he asked in his gentle, kind voice, "Would you consider moving back home with your father and family?" I had fought this question for all too long. There was a peace that came over me as I expressed my willingness and readiness to move back home. While what I experienced at this moment was different than when I first recognized I was a child of this father, I could sense in a special way that this moment was a significant marker in my life. There was a new sense of freedom, a greater sense of belonging, and a relinquishing of the fear of feeling alone. I found my source of life in this father and his provision.

The father took great joy in my decision. He committed all his and the family's resources to help me move back home. He immediately assigned a few of the family members who had accompanied me to the house to assist further my move. They were to show me around the house, teach me the household chores, teach me the house's rules, and help me move and sort through the rest of my baggage. I was surprised how every step toward and within this house had become increasingly hospitable. The father and family were always demonstrating a genuine welcome and worked to help me feel comfortable in my new surroundings.

As I moved deeper into the house, I was immediately struck by what seemed like a continual feast. The father wanted to communicate that there is abundance in his house. This abundance was not spread about wastefully, but in a manner that enabled the children to flourish. The father refused to deny his children anything they truly needed. The celebratory atmosphere, matched with this abundance, further communicated the father's delight in his children.

My newly assigned family members reassured me that it would take some time for me to grow accustomed to my new home. The family knew it was a big change for me and understood that it would take some time for me to acclimate. They started by showing me around the house. First, they showed me the essential living areas and how to navigate them. As we continued exploring, I was amazed how big this house really was! They told me that even they had not yet explored all the rooms because the house was so large.

They also shared with me that to navigate the house well all I needed to do was to follow the house rules. The house rules were simple—act in loving ways to the father and to each other. I could not believe that there were only two rules. The family members recognized how simple I thought the rules were. They assured me that soon I would see how these rules are not as easy as they first appeared.

I was already somewhat familiar with the house chores, as I had helped with some already. The family members shared that the essential house chores revolved around extending the father's hospitality to all travelers and household members, and to assist returning travelers in the same manner as I had been helped. They also recognized that I thought some of the chores were ridiculously easy. The family members warned against becoming distracted from the central chores and focusing on tasks that hindered the house's primary mission.

As more time passed, I continued to explore the house and work on the chores. Over time, I became more adept at the chores. My close family members continued to meet with me. We shared stories of our challenges and successes. We found we were able to encourage and help each other each week as we discovered new things about the father and his house. I discovered I was particularly challenged as I would make my way out on the highway to find people who might be ready to make the journey to the father's house. Sometimes, old friends would ask me to stay with them back in the old world. Other times, I would be attracted and tempted by my former way of living. Thankfully, I always traveled with my close family members. When these temptations would come, I was comfortable in sharing these moments with my family. They were able to point me back home and remind me of my father's love. As I have grown and found healing, I am thankful that the father invited me to live with him in his house.

The House		God's Action	Location	Steps to the House of God
Works of Mercy - Feeding, Clothing, Visiting				Profound Love for Others
Anger				Profound Love for God
Works of Justice				Loves enemies, Loves Strangers
Racism	The King's Highway	Sanctifying Grace	Moving home with God and immersing myself in the presence of God continually.	Displays Consistent Biblical Hospitality
Fasting				Goes out to Help Travelers
Division				Active in Bringing the Kingdom of God
Fearful of Change				Producing Fruit of the Spirit
Lack of Humility				Stewardship of all Resources
Searching Scriptures				Engages in House Chores - Make Disciples
Greed				Learns House Rules - Love God, Love Others
Perfectionism				Self Denial
Worship				Picks up Cross
Fear				Willing to Surrender All to God
Eucharist				No Longer Hiding from God
Sin				Recognizes a Need to Love Others More
Prayer				Desire for More of God
Class Meeting				Broken by God
Potential Blockages, Barriers, and Baggage and the Means of Grace to Move Barriers				Steps to the House of God

	= Barriers, Blockages, and Baggage
	= Means of Grace

Analysis of the Map

The preceding story and map of the house (figure 11) sets the stage for this chapter. The story gives a personal yet practical feeling as to what is taking place in this area of God's house. The map is designed to provide a general layout of what it looks like to move into and dwell in God's house. This map is not to be seen as a checklist to be marked off in a subsequent order: steps may be combined, completed out of order, or there may be additional steps not elaborated in this map. Ultimately, every individual experiences God's grace differently.

There are some significant steps enumerated in this map. These steps include: producing the fruit of the Spirit, self-denial, no longer hiding from God, learning the house rules, and engaging in the house chores. There are other significant transformational steps illustrated in this map as well. Many of these steps are not instantaneous actions but occur over a lifetime as one's relationship with God deepens. Some steps may need to be repeated, at different periods of life. This stage strongly emphasizes "being" over "doing." If the relational discipler focuses with the disciple on "being" as opposed to focusing on a list of rules, then the disciple will live more intentionally for God and experience greater transformation.

In this area of God's house, God's prior action is experienced as sanctifying grace. We will recall that in chapter 2 on grace that I explained God has only one grace but that our transformation can recognize God's grace acting in different ways in our lives. We also established that all of God's grace is prevenient in that God always acts first in every moment of our lives, enabling us to choose the most loving option available in that moment.[1] Our responsibility is to recognize God's grace in each moment, and then to choose the most loving option we have available at that time. When we can say that love motivates all of our choices, we can then say we are living in perfect love.[2]

We have often confused crisis experiences with how sanctifying grace functions in the Christian's daily life. Wesley cautioned against undue emphasis upon experience. In his Large Minutes, Wesley wrote this question and answer:

---

1. Oord, *Love*, 129.
2. Clapper, *Heart*, 71.

Q.35. Why are not we more holy? Why do not we love in eternity? Walk with God all the day long? Why are we not all devoted to God? Breathing the whole spirit of missionaries?

A. Because we are enthusiasts, looking for the end without using the means.[3]

If an experience is the focus of our faith, we fail to anticipate how God's sanctifying grace *continually* operates in our lives. We fail to recognize the importance of the faithful practice of the means of grace. God's sanctifying grace is not something we experience only once. Rather, God's sanctifying grace operates *throughout* our lives, moving us closer to God.[4]

Our map illustrates potential other hindrances a disciple can experience on the journey to God's house. The relational discipler must faithfully listen as the disciple continually confesses her journey. In the confession of her story, we should be sensitive to listen for those things that encumber and block her recognition of and response to God's grace. A disciple may not experience any of the suggested barriers, blockages, or baggage our map illustrates. The hindrances the disciple experiences can come from barriers the church erects limiting access to God's abundant grace, blockages that the world uses to try and disrupt one's way back to God, or baggage that the disciple has brought along the journey from past experiences.

We will notice that fewer hindrances appear on this particular map than in previous maps. This fact can be attributed to the faithful practice of additional means of grace as I mentioned in chapter 8 on the door. Prayerfully, the accountable practice of additional means of grace will help alleviate hindrances to God's grace. The disciple may employ the means of grace prayerfully on behalf of the new disciple. Conversely, the new disciple may use the means of grace to facilitate spiritual growth. Building upon the previous transformation, the relational discipler will engage, teach, and model the appropriate means of grace illustrated in this map. Even if a particular means of grace was taught and practiced in the previous map, further development in the understanding and practice of each particular means of grace could be explored.

---

3. Enthusiasm in Wesley's day was not a positive term. It's root means being taken over by a spirit, not necessarily God's. In other words, we would say "unbridled fanaticism." Also see Wesley's sermon on enthusiasm, J. Wesley, *The Works of John Wesley*, vol. 5, 467.

4. J. Wesley, *The Works of John Wesley*, vol. 6, 1.

Notice that the further a disciple goes into the house of God, the more outward focused her practice of the means of grace become. For instance, we will see that works of justice and works of mercy on behalf of others occur in locations of profound love for God and others. One could argue that these outwardly focused means of grace could be implemented earlier in the map of the house in order to develop a profound love for God and others. Prayerful sensitivity for the direction of the Holy Spirit should be the guide for the decision in directing the practice of any new means of grace.

The means of grace in this particular location will also increasingly focus on self-denial. John Wesley considered the lack of self-denial to be the greatest threat to Methodism.[5] Previously, the means of grace were centrally focused on the needs and development of the disciple. The means of grace, in sanctifying grace, become focused on God and others. For example, scripture reading becomes less about feeding the disciple's soul, and more about learning to know and love God. Worship becomes less of a focus on an individual feeling, and more on adoring the God, who has provided a steadfast love.

Fasting is another important means of grace that the church has often made optional. For Wesley, fasting was a means of grace that provided a practical way of reminding oneself of the importance of denial and a practical way of disciplining the physical body.[6] In the Introduction of this resource, I indicated that the means of grace in relational discipleship is more about knowing God and others in all ways that there is to know others and not just about having knowledge of the other. By reducing the focus on self, the means of grace, in conjunction with sanctifying grace, work together to enable the believer to know and love God and others.

Hospitality remains central to the relational discipleship process. The relational discipler will continue to build upon the previous stages of hospitality. Once one enters God's house, hospitality develops into a mode of sending forth. The lines will still be blurred, and other stages of hospitality will need to be reinforced. The features of welcoming, restoring, and dwelling will need to be addressed depending on the disciple and her experience. However, as the disciple begins to experience sanctifying grace, the relational discipler will see the need for the disciple to join and to go forth

---

5. J. Wesley, *The Works of John Wesley*, vol. 6, 103. Also see, J. Wesley, *The Works of John Wesley*, vol. 7, 288. Also see, J. Wesley, *The Works of John Wesley*, vol. 13, 258.

6. J. Wesley, *The Works of John Wesley*, vol. 6, 51. Also see, J. Wesley, *The Works of John Wesley*, vol. 8, 274, 364.

in mission. Sanctifying grace does not allow one to remain self-focused. Sanctifying grace invites one to reach out, deny oneself, and love God and others extravagantly.

In this stage of hospitality, the relational discipler should focus on extending key traits of hospitality that enable and facilitate mission. Again, previous key traits will continue to be addressed in the discipling process, depending on the continuing needs of the disciple. A relational discipler will continue to exhibit gift giving and generosity, risk taking, reducing strangeness, creating a safe environment, promise keeping, friendship, and celebration. In this stage, a greater degree of truthfulness can be both shared and expected between the discipler and disciple.[7] The class meeting experience will prayerfully have provided by this stage a deep desire to be truthful and the ability to share the truth—both in the truthfulness of where one has come and the truthfulness in the direction one should go.

This truthfulness can only flourish as the relational discipler reinforces the key trait of hospitality that the outcome belongs to God. A discipler can be patient and accepting of the truthfulness of where one has come and is now on the journey because the discipler trusts the outcome to God. The discipler does not have to take upon oneself the responsibility to effect the change in a disciple. A discipler does not have to be frustrated, discouraged, or feel like a failure because of the disciple's perceived slow and uneven transformation. Additionally, the disciple can be confident that God is the source of her transformation. She can take confidence that God will continue to work until the work is completed (Philippians 1:6). As the disciple seeks to be transformed into an agent of God's perfect love, she need not be discouraged by the lack of progress. Her confidence is in God who is on the journey with her.

As with every location on the journey back to God's house, the cycle of resistance to God's grace should always be anticipated to some degree. However, the further one moves into God's house, the cycle of resistance should be less demonstrative. God's grace, as it lures us toward God, always creates discontent with the change that we recognize must occur in our lives to respond to God's grace. It is when we do not wrestle with and come to terms with this change that God's grace is compelling that we become complacent to God and even stalled in our transformation. Relational disciplers, because of their own struggle with the further calls of God's grace

---

7. I am using terms that correspond to the key traits outlined in chapter three on hospitality.

in their lives, are in danger of allowing other travelers to stall in their transformation. Discipler and disciple both need to recognize their tendency to resist God's grace, and need to recognize proper ways to reduce these hindrances as they seek to be transformed by God's grace into the people they should be.

At this point, the relational discipler will either hinder or facilitate the disciple's growth. This location will depend on the authentic sharing of the relational discipler's own experienced cycles of resistance. In this stage of the house, the resistance does not have to be outright disobedience or rage but simply a confession that God is inviting some growth and change that is causing some discomfort. Such honesty will provide a healthy context for the disciple to confront her own struggles with God's grace.

As always, the cycle of receiving and experiencing God's grace can be understood in the context of gratitude and gift giving. A relational discipler recognizes the positive response to God's grace when a disiciple exhibits a life characterized by gratitude toward God. Conversely, a disciple whose spiritual growth has stalled will cease to demonstrate gratitude toward God. Gratitude is an important indication of one's spiritual health and life.

Additionally, gratitude always produces a spirit of gift giving. One who positively responds to God's grace will exhibit gratitude that flows into gifting that same grace to others around her. The work of God or the mission of God should not be understood as tedious or demanding. A disciple who is responding positively to God's grace will generally live a life where God's grace flows abundantly through her. Obviously, spiritual growth is not always consistent. However, a relational discipler can observe how a disciple shares grace with others as an indication of her spiritual growth.

Moving into God's house is a lifelong process. This process is also a moment to moment experience of the awareness of the transforming presence and grace of God. At some moments, we are more responsive to God. At other moments, we do not respond as well as we should. Therefore, moving into God's house is best accomplished with the help of other family members who help us move into God's presence. While we do not earn salvation by the means of grace, we find that the means of grace help us to recognize and grab hold of God's grace while at the same time removing hindrances that interfere with our response to God's grace. In this location of God's house, we find that relational discipleship impacts how we know and relate to God and others. We find that in this location, we always see more profound demonstrations of perfect love. These demonstrations lure us to move toward reflecting and acting in similar ways. We repent that we have not loved in those ways and are lured to love as we have been loved. God comes to where we are at and walks the distance with us, to enable us to love in these perfect ways. The journey into God's house is ever before us as we are always lured to move closer in God and to others.

The End of the Trail

In the preceding pages, I have laid out a path for spiritual formation that I call relational discipleship. I started the journey by considering how the church has traditionally made disciples. I enumerated the areas where these discipleship models fail to achieve the expectations of Christ regarding the discipleship of others (Matthew 28:19–20). I explained that the model I propose depended upon relational and Wesleyan theology. John Wesley's ecclesiology factors importantly into this relational concept. It places a premium on knowing God and others (right-relatedness) and less on the knowledge of God and others (right beliefs). This foundation provided the direction in which the relational discipleship journey traveled.

With this starting point, we explored each progressive step in how this model impacts our view of and interaction with God. The first place we visited was an understanding of God and creation. This location explained God's "reigning attribute" of love.[8] We took a look at creation and God's desire for creation. We found that God wanted to be relationally involved with God's creation. In this relationship, human beings expressed their free will in ways that interrupted the good relationship between God, people, and each other. God, through Jesus Christ, worked to bring healing back

---

8. Wynkoop, *Theology*, 70. From Wesley's *Notes on the Bible*, "4:8 God is love-This little sentence brought St. John more sweetness, even in the time he was writing it, than the whole world can bring. God is often styled holy, righteous, wise; but not holiness, righteousness, or wisdom in the abstract, as he is said to be love; intimating that this is his darling, his reigning attribute, the attribute that sheds an amiable glory on all his other perfections." http://wesley.nnu.edu/john-wesley/john-wesleys-notes-on-the-bible/notes-on-the-first-epistle-of-st-john/#Chapter+IV , (accessed on August 29, 2015).

to creation and to restore and reconcile the alienated relationship with humanity. Eventually, God will redeem all of creation when God fully returns to this world.

We then proceeded to move a little further on our journey. Here, we explored grace—God's loving action and presence in the world. We defined God's grace as always being prevenient—always acting prior to any of our actions. We saw that through this grace, God did not desire just to overlook our poor ways of relating to others. God desired to heal and to transform us by God's grace. We experience this transformation through justifying and sanctifying grace. God extends justifying grace to demonstrate to us that we have always been God's children, but that we need to accept the grace that God freely gives. Sanctifying grace is the grace that invites us continually to go further toward God and in God, and to express perfect love toward God and others. It is crucial to understand God's grace as both universal and optimistic. God wants all people to experience abundant life through God's grace.

In this location, I noted how a relational discipler can use the cycle of grace to observe the spiritual health of the disciple. This cycle always begins with God's grace, proceeds to the recipient's gratitude for grace, and then results in her turning around and gifting that grace to others. Within this cycle of grace, we also noted the possibility of the disciple experiencing the cycle of resisting God's grace. All of us resist God's grace to some degree. The only difference is that typically, a more mature disciple will find the resistance to be more minimal in her walk. Resistance begins when one experiences God's compelling invitation to move forward in grace. With this invitation, one experiences some level of discontent. As one deals with the implications in a healthy manner, one can move toward grief as she comes to terms with the change to which God is calling one. Grief will turn to the praise of God once the person accepts and begins the journey in this new direction. Both the cycle of grace and cycle of resistance to grace can be indicators of a disciple's spiritual health and location.

From grace, we moved on to focus on the importance of hospitality. We saw that God's grace operates through hospitality. God always invites and never coerces. God welcomes the stranger, the enemy, the sick, and the marginalized. We saw that relational discipleship focuses on four stages of hospitality: the welcome, restoration, dwelling with, and sending forth.

There are also key traits of hospitality that enable and reinforce these four stages. A relational discipler will focus intentionally on exhibiting these key traits in a lifestyle of hospitality. Relational discipleship is practiced through a lifestyle and attitude of genuine biblical hospitality expressed by the relational discipler.

As we proceeded down the relational discipleship journey, our next step was to explore the class meeting. The class meeting is a primary means of grace in the relational discipleship model. This means of grace enables the relational discipler to help the disciple overcome hindrances to God's grace that I defined as barriers the church erects, blockages the world attempts to disrupt with, and baggage that the disciple carries from life experiences.[9] These hindrances are overcome through the accountable practice of the means of grace that are taught and modeled in the class meeting.

A cycle perpetually exists in a disciple's life. It consists of Wesley's pillars of doctrine: repentance, faith, and holiness. As one experiences perfect love or holiness in God or others, the person develops an awareness of the need to exhibit perfect love. Perfect love attracts the person to want to move toward and to exhibit this love. This change in mind is what we call repentance. At the moment one decides to move toward this perfect love, God comes alongside this person and gifts faith so that this person can move in that direction. The person then begins to exhibit this perfect love or holiness. This cycle continually repeats itself in the disciple's life.

We now proceed to our next stop, which is understanding this movement as degrees of faith. We explored the difference between crisis experiences and small transformational steps. We discovered that people will experience both types of transformation. However, we should not expect cookie cutter experiences that match our personal experiences or occur in our conception of time. While there will be crisis moments, we also should expect many smaller steps between each crisis moment. We learned the importance of viewing transformation as slow and uneven.

The final chapters, 6 through 9, explored the relational discipleship model through the analogy of Wesley's house of religion. We explored the woods, the porch, the door, and the house. In each location, I explained that while the map is a good reference, it should not be looked to as a precise checklist. The maps also generally outline hindrances to God's grace and the means of grace that help to overcome those hindrances. These locations

---

9. I began the description of these hindrances in chapter four on the class meeting and continued the development in the chapters that followed.

enable a relational discipler to locate and extend hospitality to each disciple as she travels toward God. The analogy of the house also demonstrates the importance of beginning discipleship with one who has begun to be awakened, and not to reserve discipleship exclusively to those who have already experienced justifying grace.

As we conclude, some may think that I have complicated the discipleship process or tried to wrap it tightly in some box that can be controlled. I think I have done just the opposite. I have tried to depict a process of discipleship that matches scripture, tradition, reason, and experience. At the same time, I have intentionally left lines blurred and have cautioned against stereotyping the process. I have noted how there is latitude in how and when growth occurs at each stage.

I would like to take the remainder of this chapter and explore some potential objections:

Works Oriented

Some might object that I am proposing a model that emphasizes a works oriented salvation. I will confess that the means of grace are important components of relational discipleship and transformation. However, I indicated in chapter 5 on the degrees of faith, that American Christianity has inadvertently overloaded justification.[10] Justification is overloaded when the church communicates that one must embrace certain ways of living or believing to be "saved." In chapter 8, on the door, I again reinforce that justification is simply embracing and understanding that we have always been children of God. The means of grace that I propose in this model help to open us up to justification, and to the full salvation God wants to effect in our lives as we positively respond to God's grace in each moment.

This Discipleship Model is Not the Way We Have Done it

I have argued that our typical models have not maximized our discipleship efforts. I argued in the introduction that there are typically two models that today's church utilizes. The first model emphasizes having the right beliefs, knowledge, or doctrines. This model typically focuses on Bible studies and the communication of right beliefs. The other model is consumerism,

---

10. Watson, *Foreclose*, 108.

where each person is focused on their own needs. If a person feels she is not being fed, then she feels free to leave the church to find another congregation where her needs will be met. My goal was to provide intentionally a different model from the one we have been utilizing in the hope that we can do better at making disciples.

People Don't Want Accountability

An authentic concern is whether people will be willing to be held accountable by others. Most people are uncomfortable with being held accountable by others. The only way to address this concern appropriately is by integrating accountability with hospitality (see chapter 3 on hospitality). When patience and hospitality are experienced, people will become more comfortable in an accountability group. This comfort will not occur immediately. The process takes time. The relational discipler will also have to model genuine accountability. As accountability is modeled, people will find a safe place to begin to confess their stories. Finally, accountability does not mean judgment. People should be challenged rather than interrogated. People should be encouraged to share as deeply as they can each week in a safe environment.

Minimalizing Crisis Experiences

Depending on one's tradition, it could be suggested that this model minimizes crisis experiences. If we refer back to chapter 5 on the degrees of faith, we will then find that I embrace both crisis experiences and a journey of smaller steps. If we are honest with ourselves, then we can recognize the truth of gradual spiritual development. Additionally, we will also recognize that if spiritual growth occurs over time, then progressive development is more common than crisis experiences. This is not to deny, however, the importance of crisis experiences in our Christian walk.

Final Thoughts

We find ourselves coming to the end of this particular journey only to find another journey confronting us. As we come to the last few pages of this journey, we must ask ourselves what we will do with relational discipleship.

I have outlined a compelling story and vehicle for engaging discipleship more effectively. You may have never been exposed to relational or Wesleyan theology. Please do not focus on labels. Consider the process presented and the potential it has for real transformation.

Evaluate your current discipleship model and efforts. Are you currently discipling intentionally? What are the fruits if you are? If you are discipling, are there any obstacles? How are people responding? Could relational discipleship give you a fuller understanding and approach? If you are not currently discipling, then what are your plans for making disciples? What is holding you back? What barriers are you experiencing at beginning to disciple others? Could you commit to engaging a relational discipleship model for a period of time to see what the impact could be?

"Go and make disciples."—Jesus (Matthew 28:19)

Postscript

Many times, people give advice and outline great strategies without personally ever having implemented these same suggestions. First, I would like to share that churches are increasingly finding accountable discipleship groups to be an effective means of discipling others. You can find resources in my bibliography that cite firsthand accounts and examples of these experiences. However, I would like to share my personal experience with developing the relational discipleship model.

A little over three years ago, one of the members of Wadsworth Church of the Nazarene felt a need for a different kind of venue to reach unchurched people. As he observed our traditional worship services and Sunday School, he concluded that many unchurched people did not feel at home in these settings. These traditional services have been what the church has always done. The problem is that many visitors would come and go and never stay. Some would finally settle in, get involved, and seek transformation through Jesus Christ. However, the majority of the visitors moved on to somewhere else.

Additionally, this particular individual is very outgoing and is continually inviting people to church. He saw that many of the people to whom he was reaching out were on the margins of life. They did not fit well into a church community. Their lives were very different from the people worshipping in the traditional settings. Occasionally, one of these people would come to church and realize they did not fit in. Most of these people had never attended traditional services.

With his vision and passion, the Sunday School launched an alternative time of fellowship. We call it Saturday Night Connect. It is an informal meal with a devotional and fellowship time. People from all ages and walks of life come together as equal members of the family to connect with each other and God. Each week we serve people with disabilities, addictions, identity issues, emotional and financial struggles, and family problems by sharing a meal with them. People who are not familiar with the story of God and do not understand "proper" ways of coming to church and behaving in church come eagerly to spend time with us.

These past three years have been rewarding, as we have seen people respond to God's grace. The transformation is slow. The transformation does not match the instantaneous cookie-cutter responses to grace that the long time church members expect. On occasion, those being ministered to through Saturday Night Connect have attended church functions and traditional services. Some long time church members have expressed concerns about these people. These long time members think that we should impose change upon the Connect people. Some of these long-time church members think we are not preaching the wrath and judgment of God enough so that these Connect people experience transformation in the time and pattern the traditional people expect and or have experienced. Needless to say, some of the long time church members have a difficult time extending hospitality to people from Connect.

Over the course of about three years, attendance at Connect has been as high as 124 and has averaged over 70 people each week. From a Wesleyan perspective, Connect has become analogous with John Wesley's field preaching. Connect is where people become awakened to God. People can hear and learn about God in a non-threatening environment.

As a result, I have been considering the implications of relational discipleship. In my particular tribe—called the Church of the Nazarene, an error has been to overemphasize two instantaneous works of grace, backed up with private discipleship and corporate transfer of knowledge. We have pushed cookie cutter responses to grace without considering the importance of relational discipleship to help people navigate and respond to God's grace. Additionally, in our concern to be a "holiness movement", we have been overly concerned about protecting our identity, and failed to understand what biblical hospitality means.

Relational Discipleship

As Connect continued to develop, and I delved deeper into my studies in Wesleyan practices, the leaders of Connect started becoming aware that there was a need for the next step in discipleship for the people attending Connect. A re-traditioned class meeting became the apparent next step. We began praying and searching out how a class meeting would look and be implemented. We decided to call the class meeting "Grace Group." At our weekly Connect time, we started explaining what this Grace Group was. We explained that the Grace Group would be a group that would meet each week with the explicit purpose of looking for and responding to God's grace. We asked people to fill out a short form expressing an interest in being part of this group.

After three months of sharing about the Grace Group, we had 12 people join the group. We began meeting an hour before Connect each Saturday. Because most of the people who had responded had no church background, we started with the very basics of teaching people about Wesley's analogy of the House of Religion. People learned how prevenient, justifying, and sanctifying grace corresponded to the porch, door, and house respectively. People learned that in each moment, God was extending grace to each person and that each person had a responsibility to respond to God's grace.

The members of this Grace Group were asked to examine their lives with the help of the Holy Spirit and to recognize where they were in relation to God's house. Were they lost in the woods? Were they trying to live their own way in their own broken down shacks? Were they sitting on the porch, learning who God is? Had they accepted God's invitation, made possible by Jesus Christ, to walk through the door of the house? Were they willing to move into God's house and live in God's presence continually, moment by moment? Each person shared where he or she thought they were at that particular moment in relation to God's house.

We then set out in the following weeks to write a covenant for our Grace Group. This covenant consisted of actual means of grace to which we would all try to engage in each week. The covenant is based upon David Lowes Watson's suggestion of having equal means of grace activities for all four types of means of grace—acts of justice, compassion, devotion, and worship.[11] After the covenant had been written, we celebrated one Saturday by signing the covenant together and closing with the Eucharist.

---

11. Watson, *Covenant*, 116.

We now meet each week to respond to different questions posed by the class leader as to how we have been keeping the covenant. More importantly, since the covenant and the activities of the covenant are means of grace, we have proceeded to the question of how we have seen and responded to God's grace each week. Every person gives a report of how they and God are relating. We encourage one another, challenge one another, and pray for one another.

Teaching Wesleyan practices in the context of the Grace Group has enlivened the holiness message within our Connect group. Holiness is more about learning to live in God's presence moment by moment and less about which negative actions to avoid. This process has demonstrated that God wants to transform us into Christ's image here and now. We are learning in Grace Group that it is God's presence, God's grace that transforms us. It is by practicing the means of grace that we learn to see and respond to God's grace. We are excited to be helping each other move into God's house. Further plans are being made to implement additional grace groups including groups for our traditional church gathering.

Appendix A

The General Rules and Rules of the Band-Societies

The Nature, Design, and General Rules of the United Societies

IN LONDON, BRISTOL, KINGSWOOD, NEWCASTLE-UPON-TYNE, &c.

1. IN the latter end of the year 1739, eight or ten persons came to me in London, who appeared to be deeply convinced of sin, and earnestly groaning for redemption. They desired (as did two or three more the next day) that I would spend some time with them in prayer, and advise them how to flee from the wrath to come; which they saw continually hanging over their heads. That we might have more time for this great work, I appointed a day when they might all come together, which from thenceforward they did every week, namely, on Thursday, in the evening. To these, and as many more as desired to join with them, (for their number increased daily,) I gave those advices, from time to time, which I judged most needful for them; and we always concluded our meeting with prayer suited to their several necessities.

2. This was the rise of the United Society, first in London, and then in other places. Such a society is no other than "a company of men having the form and seeking the power of godliness, united in order to pray together, to receive the word of exhortation, and to watch over one another in love, that they may help each other to work out their salvation."

3. That it may the more easily be discerned, whether they are indeed working out their own salvation, each society is divided into smaller

companies, called classes, according to their respective places of abode. There are about twelve persons in every class; one of whom is styled the Leader. It is his business, (1.) To see each person in his class once a week at least, in order to inquire how their souls prosper; to advise, reprove, comfort, or exhort, as occasion may require; to receive what they are willing to give toward the relief of the poor. (2.) To meet the Minister and the Stewards of the society once a week; in order to inform the Minister of any that are sick, or of any that walk disorderly, and will not be reproved; to pay to the Stewards what they have received of their several classes in the week preceding; and to show their account of what each person has contributed.

4. There is one only condition previously required in those who desire admission into these societies,—a desire "to flee from the wrath to come, to be saved from their sins:" But, wherever this is really fixed in the soul, it will be shown by its fruits. It is therefore expected of all who continue therein, that they should continue to evidence their desire of salvation,

    First, by doing no harm, by avoiding evil in every kind; especially that which is most generally practised: Such is, the taking the name of God in vain; the profaning the day of the Lord, either by doing ordinary work thereon, or by buying or selling; drunkenness, buying or selling spirituous liquors, or drinking them, unless in cases of extreme necessity; fighting, quarreling, brawling; brother going to law with brother; returning evil for evil, or railing for railing; the using many words in buying or selling; the buying or selling uncustomed goods; the giving or taking things on usury, that is, unlawful interest; uncharitable or unprofitable conversation, particularly speaking evil of Magistrates or of Ministers; doing to others as we would not they should do unto us; doing what we know is not for the glory of God, as the "putting on of gold or costly apparel;" the taking such diversions as cannot be used in the name of the Lord Jesus; the singing those songs, or reading those books, which do not tend to the knowledge or love of God; softness, and needless self-indulgence; laying up treasures upon earth; borrowing without a probability of paying; or taking up goods without a probability of paying for them.

5. It is expected of all who continue in these societies, that they should continue to evidence their desire of salvation,

Secondly, by doing good, by being, in every kind, merciful after their power; as they have opportunity, doing good of every possible sort, and as far as is possible, to all men;—to their bodies, of the ability which God giveth, by giving food to the hungry, by clothing the naked, by visiting or helping them that are sick, or in prison;—to their souls, by instructing reproving, or exhorting all they have any intercourse with; trampling under foot that enthusiastic doctrine of devils, that "we are not to do good unless our heart be free to it:" By doing good especially to them that are of the household of faith, or groaning so to be; employing them preferably to others, buying one of another; helping each other in business; and so much the more, because the world will love its own, and them only: By all possible diligence and frugality, that the gospel be not blamed: By running with patience the race that is set before them, "denying themselves, and taking up their cross daily;" submitting to bear the reproach of Christ, to be as the filth and offscouring of the world; and looking that men should "say all manner of evil of them falsely for the Lord's sake."

6. It is expected of all who desire to continue in these societies, that they should continue to evidence their desire of salvation,

    Thirdly, by attending upon all the ordinances of God. Such are, the public worship of God; the ministry of the word, either read or expounded; the supper of the Lord; family and private prayer; searching the Scriptures; and fasting, or abstinence.

7. These are the General Rules of our societies; all which we are taught of God to observe, even in his written word, the only rule, and the sufficient rule, both of our faith and practice. And all these, we know, his Spirit writes on every truly awakened heart. If there be any among us who observe them not, who habitually break any of them, let it be made known unto them who watch over that soul as they that must give an account. We will admonish him of the error of his ways; we will bear with him for a season: But then if he repent not, he hath no more place among us. We have delivered our own souls.

JOHN WESLEY,
CHARLES WESLEY.
May 1. 1743.

Appendix B

Rules of the Band-Societies

DRAWN UP DECEMBER 25, 1738.

THE DESIGN OF OUR meeting is, to obey that command of God, "Confess your faults one to another, and pray one for another, that ye may be healed."

To this end, we intend,—

1. To meet once a week, at the least.
2. To come punctually at the hour appointed, without some extraordinary reason.
3. To begin (those of us who are present) exactly at the hour, with singing or prayer.
4. To speak each of us in order, freely and plainly, the true state of our souls, with the faults we have committed in thought, word, or deed, and the temptations we have felt, since our last meeting.
5. To end every meeting with prayer, suited to the state of each person present.
6. To desire some person among us to speak his own state first, and then to ask the rest, in order, as many and as searching questions as may be, concerning their state, sins, and temptations.

Some of the questions proposed to every one before he is admitted among us may be to this effect:—

1. Have you the forgiveness of your sins?
2. Have you peace with God, through our Lord Jesus Christ?

Rules of the Band-Societies

3. Have you the witness of God's Spirit with your spirit, that you are a child of God?
4. Is the love of God shed abroad in your heart?
5. Has no sin, inward or outward, dominion over you?
6. Do you desire to be told of your faults?
7. Do you desire to be told of all your faults, and that plain and home?
8. Do you desire that every one of us should tell you, from time to time, whatsoever is in his heart concerning you?
9. Consider! Do you desire we should tell you whatsoever we think, whatsoever we fear, whatsoever we hear, concerning you?
10. Do you desire that, in doing this, we should come as close as possible, that we should cut to the quick, and search your heart to the bottom?
11. Is it your desire and design to be on this, and all other occasions, entirely open, so as to speak everything that is in your heart without exception, without disguise, and without reserve?

Any of the preceding questions may be asked as often as occasion offers; the four following at every meeting:—

1. What known sins have you committed since our last meeting?
2. What temptations have you met with?
3. How were you delivered?
4. What have you thought, said, or done, of which you doubt whether it be sin or not?[1]

---

1. Wesley, J., "The Nature, Design, and General Rules of the United Societies, in London," The Works of John Wesley, vol. 8, 269–273.

Bibliography

Akkerman, Jay Richard, Thomas J. Oord, and Brent D. Peterson, eds. *Postmodern and Wesleyan? Exploring the Boundaries and Possibilities*. Kansas City: Beacon Hill, 2009.

Barna, George. *Maximum Faith: Live Like Jesus*. New York: Strategenius, 2011.

Barna Group. "Research on How God Transforms Lives Reveals a 10 Stop Journey." https://www.barna.org/transformation-articles/480-research-on-how-god-transforms-lives-reveals-a-10-stop-journey (accessed August 26, 2015).

Blevins, Dean G., and Mark A. Maddix. *Discovering Discipleship: Dynamics of Christian Education*. Kansas City: Beacon Hill, 2010.

Bonhoeffer, Dietrich. *The Cost of Discipleship*. New York: Touchstone, 1995.

Boren, M. Scott. *The Relational Way: From Small Group Structures to Holistic Life Connections*. Houston: TOUCH Publications, 2007.

———. *Missional Small Groups: Becoming A Community that Makes a Difference in the World*. Grand Rapids: Baker, 2010.

Boyd, Gregory A. *Repenting of Religion: Turning from Judgment to the Love of God*. Grand Rapids: Baker, 2004.

———. *Benefit of the Doubt: Breaking the Idol of Certainty*. Grand Rapids: Baker, 2013.

———. Living as if God Exists. http://reknew.org/2014/04/living-as-if-god-exists/ (accessed 04/22/2014).

Boyd, Gregory A., and Paul R. Eddy. *Across the Spectrum: Understanding Issues in Evangelical Theology*. Grand Rapids: Baker Academic, 2002.

Broward, Josh, and Thomas Jay Oord. eds. *Renovating Holiness*. Nampa: SacraSage, 2015.

Carder, Kenneth L., and Laceye C. Warner. *Grace to Lead: Practicing Leadership in the Wesleyan Tradition*. Nashville: General Board of Higher Education and Ministry, 2011.

Carson, D. A. *Becoming Conversant with the Emerging Church: Understanding a Movement and its Implications*. Grand Rapids: Zondervan, 2005.

Carson, D.A., ed. *Telling the Truth: Evangelizing Postmoderns*. Grand Rapids: Zondervan, 2000.

Clapper, Gregory S. *As If the Heart Mattered: A Wesleyan Spirituality*. Nashville: Upper Room, 1997.

Collins, Kenneth J. *The Theology of John Wesley: Holy Love and the Shape of Grace*. Nashville, TN: Abingdon, 2007.

Bibliography

Crofford, J. Gregory. *Streams of Mercy: Prevenient Grace in the Theology of John and Charles Wesley*. Lexington, KY: Emeth, 2010.

Cunningham, David S., ed. *To Teach, to Delight, and to Move: Theological Education in a Post-Christian World*. OR: Cascade, 2004.

De La Torre, Miguel A. *Reading the Bible from the Margins*. Maryknoll, NY: Orbis, 2002.

Donahue, Bill, and Russ Robinson. *Building A Church of Small Groups: A Place Where Nobody Stands Alone*. Grand Rapids: Zondervan, 2001.

———. *Walking the Small Group Tightrope: Meeting the Challenges Every Group Faces*. Grand Rapids: Zondervan, 2003.

Engel, James F., and Wilbert Norton. *What's Gone Wrong With the Harvest?: A Communication Strategy for the Church and World Evangelism*. Grand Rapids: Zondervan, 1975.

Erickson, Millard J. *Postmodernizing the Faith: Evangelical Responses to the Challenge of Postmodernism*. Grand Rapids: Baker, 1998.

———. *Truth or Consequences: The Promise and Perils of Postmodernism*. Downers Grove: InterVarsity, 2001.

———. *The Postmodern World: Discerning the Times and the Spirit of Our Age*. Wheaton: Crossway. 2002.

Foster, Richard J. *Life with God*. New York, NY: HarperCollins, 2008.

Gray, Frank. "The Gray Matrix," http://thegraymatrix.org/ (accessed on August 26, 2015).

"Greek Lexicon: G3622 (KJV)." Blue Letter Bible. Accessed 2 Sep, 2015. http://www.blueletterbible.org/lang/lexicon/lexicon.cfm?Strongs=G3622&t=KJV

Green, Joel B. *Seized by Truth*. Nashville, TN: Abingdon, 2007.

———. *Practicing Theological Interpretation*. Grand Rapids, MI: Baker Academic, 2011.

Green, Joel B., and Jeffrey E. Greenway, eds. *Grace and Holiness in a Changing World: A Wesleyan Proposal for Postmodern Ministry*. Nashville: Abingdon, 2007.

Greer, Robert C. *Mapping Postmodernism: A Survey of Christian Options*. Downers Grove, IL: InterVarsity, 2003.

Harford, Fabs. Knowing God or Knowing About God. *Verge*. http://www.vergenetwork.org/2014/02/19/knowing-god-or-knowing-about-god/ (accessed 04/22/2014).

Harper, Steve. *The Way to Heaven: The Gospel According to John Wesley*. Grand Rapids: Zondervan, 2003.

"Hebrew Lexicon: H1481 (NIV)." Blue Letter Bible. Accessed 24 Aug, 2015. http://www.blueletterbible.org/lang/lexicon/lexicon.cfm?Strongs=H1481&t=NIV

Horton, Florence. "Walking in the King's Highway" (No. 519) in *Sing to the Lord*. Kansas City: Lillenas, 1993.

Heuertz, Christopher L., and Christine D. Pohl. *Friendship at the Margins: Discovering Mutuality in Service and Mission*. Downers Grove: Inter Varsity, 2010.

Hull, Bill. *The Complete Book of Discipleship: On Being and Making Followers of Christ*. Colorado Springs: NavPress, 2006.

Hunter III, George G. *To Spread the Power: Church Growth in the Wesleyan Spirit*. Nashville, TN: Abingdon, 1987.

Hunter III, George G. *Radical Outreach: The Recovery of Apostolic Ministry and Evangelism*. Nashville, TN: Abingdon, 2003.

———. *The Presence of God in the Christian Life: John Wesley and the Means of Grace*. Metuchen, NJ: Scarecrow, 1992.

Lodahl, Michael. *God of Nature and Grace: Reading the World in a Wesleyan Way*. Nashville: Kingswood, 2003.

Bibliography

Maddox, Randy L. *Responsible Grace: John Wesley's Practical Theology*. Nashville: Kingswood, 1994.
Manskar, Steven W., *Accountable Discipleship: Living in God's Household*. Nashville: Discipleship Resources, 2006.
Manskar, Steven W., Marjorie H. Suchocki, and Diana L. Hynson. *A Perfect Love: Understanding John Wesley's A Plain Account of Christian Perfection*. Nashville: Discipleship Resources, 2004.
Matthaei, Sondra Higgins. *Making Disciples*. Nashville, TN: Abingdon, 2000.
McGonigle, Herbert Boyd. *Sufficient Saving Grace: John Wesley's Evangelical Arminianism*. Waynesboro, GA: Paternoster, 2001.
Meeks, M. Douglas. *God the Economist: The Doctrine of God and Political Economy*. Minneapolis: Ausburg Fortress, 1989.
Montgomery, Brint, Thomas Jay Oord, and Karen Winslow, eds. *Relational Theology: A Contemporary Introduction*. Eugene: Wipf and Stock, 2012.
Munger, Robert Boyd. *My Heart Christ's Home*. Downers Grover: InterVarsity, 2001.
Nouwen, Henri J.M. *The Return of the Prodigal Son: A Story of Homecoming*. New York: Doubleday, 1992.
———. *Home Tonight: Further Reflections on the Parable of the Prodigal Son*. New York: Doubleday, 2009.
O'Connell, Maureen H. *Compassion: Loving Our Neighbor in an Age of Globalization*. Maryknoll, New York: Orbis, 2009.
Oden, Amy G., ed. *And You Welcomed Me: A Sourcebook on Hospitality in Early Christianity*. Nashville: Abingdon, 2001.
———. *God's Welcome: Hospitality for a Gospel-Hungry World*. Cleveland: Pilgrim, 2008.
Oh, Gwang Seok. *John Wesley's Ecclesiology*. Lanham, MD: Scarecrow, 2008.
Oord, Thomas J. *The Nature of Love*. St. Louis, Missouri: Chalice, 2010.
———. *The Uncontrolling Love of God: An Open and Relational Account of Providence*. Downers Grove: Inter Varsity, 2015.
Outler, Albert C. ed. *John Wesley*. New York: Oxford University Press, 1964.
Payne, William P. *American Methodism: Past and Future Growth*. Lexington, KY: Emeth, 2013.
Pinnock, Clark H., ed. *Grace Unlimited*. Eugene, OR: Wipf and Stock, 1998.
Pohl, Christine D. *Making Room: Recovering Hospitality as a Christian Tradition*. Grand Rapids: Eerdmans, 1999.
———. *Living into Community: Cultivating Practices that Sustain Us*. Grand Rapids: Eerdmans, 2012.
Raschke, Carl. *The Next Reformation: Why Evangelicals Must Embrace Postmodernity*. Grand Rapids: Baker Academic, 2004.
Rakestraw, Robert V. "John Wesley as a Theologian of Grace." *Journal of The Evangelical Theological Society* 27, no. 2 (June 1, 1984) 193–203. ATLASerials, Religion Collection, EBSCO*host* (accessed November 6, 2013).
Reist, Irwin W. "John Wesley's View of Man: A Study in Free Grace Versus Free Will." *Wesleyan Theological Journal* 7, no. 1 (January 1, 1972) 25–35. ATLASerials, Religion Collection, EBSCO*host* (accessed November 6, 2013).
Reuteler, Jim. Heart of Methodism. http://jim.reuteler.org/writings/books/heart-of-methodism/03-salvation.pdf (accessed April 24, 2014).
Richards, Lawrence O. *The Teachers Commentary*. Wheaton: Victor, 2000.
Seedbed, "About," http://seedbed.com/about-4/ (accessed August 26, 2015)

Bibliography

Smith, James K. A. *Desiring the Kingdom: Worship, Worldview, and Cultural Formation.* Grand Rapids: Baker Academic, 2009.

Smith, R. Scott. *Truth and the New Kind of Christian: The Emerging Effects of Postmodernism in the Church.* Wheaton: Crossway, 2005.

Snyder, Howard A. *Salvation Means Creation Healed: The Ecology of Sin and Grace.* Eugene: Cascade, 2011.

Stone, Bryan P. and Thomas Jay Oord, eds. *Thy Nature and Thy Name Is Love: Wesleyan and Process Theolgies in Dialogue.* Nashville, TN: Kingswood, 2001.

Walt, J.D. "Step 33: Let People Go Away Sad," in *The Daily Text: Becoming People of One Book,* http://dailytext.seedbed.com/2015/03/23/step-33-let-people-go-away-sad/ (accessed August 26, 2015).

Walton, John H. *The NIV Application Commentary: From Biblical Text to Contemporary Life.* Grand Rapids: Zondervan, 2001.

Watson, David Lowes. *God Does Not Foreclose: The Universal Promise of Salvation.* Nashville: Abingdon, 1990.

———. *Class Leaders: Recovering a Tradition.* Eugene, Wipf and Stock, 1998a.

———. *Covenant Discipleship: Christian Formation through Mutual Accountability.* Eugene: Wipf and Stock, 1998b.

———. *The Early Methodist Class Meeting: Its Origins and Significance.* Eugene: Wipf and Stock, 2002a.

———. *Forming Christian Disciples: The Role of Covenant Discipleship and Class Leaders in the Congregation.* Eugene: Wipf and Stock, 2002b.

Watson, Kevin M. *A Blueprint for Discipleship: Wesley's General Rules as a Guide for Christian Living.* Nashville, TN: Discipleship Resources, 2001.

———. *The Class Meeting: Reclaiming a Forgotten (and Essential) Small Group Experience.* Wilmore, KY: Seedbed, 2014.

Wesley, J. *Notes on the Bible.* http://wesley.nnu.edu/john-wesley/john-wesleys-notes-on-the-bible/notes-on-the-first-epistle-of-st-john/#Chapter+IV, 1754.

Wesley, J. *The Works of John Wesley.* Third Edition. London: Wesleyan Methodist Book Room, 1872.

Willimon, William H. *Bishop: The Art of Questioning Authority by an Authority in Question.* Nashville: Abingdon, 2012.

Wilson, Ira B. "Make Me a Blessing" (No. 533) in *Sing to the Lord.* Kansas City: Lillenas, 1993.

Wood, A. Skevington. *The Burning Heart John Wesley: Evangelist.* Australia: Emu Book Agencies Pty., Ltd, 1967.

Wright, N.T. *Paul and the Faithfulness of God.* Minneapolis: Fortress, 2013.

Wolsey, Roger. A Progressive Christian View of Sin and Sinners. http://www.patheos.com/blogs/rogerwolsey/2014/03/a-progressive-christian-view-of-sin-sinners/ (accessed 4/22/2014).

Wynkoop, Mildred Bangs. *A Theology of Love: The Dynamic of Wesleyanism.* Kansas City: Beacon Hill, 1972.

www.ingramcontent.com/pod-product-compliance
Lightning Source LLC
Chambersburg PA
CBHW071231170426
43191CB00032B/1323